RE ORG

*how to
get it right*

STEPHEN HEIDARI-ROBINSON
SUZANNE HEYWOOD

Harvard Business Review Press

Boston, Massachusetts

Copyright 2016 Practical Reorg Ltd.
All rights reserved
Printed in the United States of America

10 9 8 7 6 5 4 3 2 1

No part of this publication may be reproduced, stored in or introduced into a retrieval system, or transmitted, in any form, or by any means (electronic, mechanical, photocopying, recording, or otherwise), without the prior permission of the publisher. Requests for permission should be directed to permissions@hbsp.harvard.edu, or mailed to Permissions, Harvard Business School Publishing, 60 Harvard Way, Boston, Massachusetts 02163.

The web addresses referenced in this book were live and correct at the time of the book's publication but may be subject to change.

Library of Congress Cataloging-in-Publication Data
Names: Heidari-Robinson, Stephen, author. | Heywood, Suzanne, author.
Title: ReOrg : how to get it right / Stephen Heidari-Robinson and Suzanne Heywood.
Description: Boston, Massachusetts : Harvard Business Review Press, [2016] | Includes index.
Identifiers: LCCN 2016019868 (print) | LCCN 2016020787 (ebook) | ISBN 9781633692237 (hardcover : alk. paper) | ISBN 9781633692244 ()
Subjects: LCSH: Corporate reorganizations--Handbooks, manuals, etc. | Industrial management--Handbooks, manuals, etc.
Classification: LCC HD38.15 .H45 2016 (print) | LCC HD38.15 (ebook) | DDC 658.4/02--dc23
LC record available at https://lccn.loc.gov/2016019868

ISBN: 9781633692237
eISBN: 9781633692244

The paper used in this publication meets the requirements of the American National Standard for Permanence of Paper for Publications and Documents in Libraries and Archives Z39.48-1992.

To our families—Neggin, Jeremy, Jonny, Lizzie, and Peter—for their huge tolerance and support throughout all the time that we have spent both reorganizing companies and thinking about how to reorganize them.

Contents

Contents

Introduction

A Practical Manual for Your Reorg

Introduction

Reorg. What emotion do you feel when you hear this word? If you feel excited, chances are you've never experienced a reorganization. Most people dread them. If you're heading one up, you'll probably agree that no other management practice consumes more of your time and attention or creates more fear and anxiety among your colleagues than a reorg. And if you're one of those employees affected, then the reorg can create paralyzing uncertainty about your future, making it next to impossible to concentrate on anything else, let alone what you need to be doing to be successful in the new environment. Reorgs always have some adverse consequences—employees get distracted from their jobs, leaders resist change, key people leave or become demotivated because they feel they have been treated unfairly—and if you take too long to navigate through these challenges, the market can change underneath you, rendering original plans irrelevant. Given the time commitment and genuine human pain of doing a reorg, there is a temptation to outsource it to others and fail to step up to the plate yourself. For all these reasons, only one in six reorgs delivers the value it is supposed to in the time expected.[1]

Yet, if you work in an organization today, it's likely that you will lead or be part of a reorganization effort. A successful reorg can be one of the best ways for companies to unlock latent value, especially in a changing business environment—which is why companies are now doing reorgs more often. If you have not yet been involved in a reorganization, you are likely to be involved soon, either as a leader or as a participant. John Ferraro, the former chief operating officer (COO) of Ernst & Young (EY) who has reorganized his own organization and seen reorgs at clients, told us: "Every company today is being disrupted and has to reorganize itself frequently to keep up with the incredible pace of change. The companies that can do this well will thrive in today's environment and will be tomorrow's winners."

We've written this book to help executives do just that—get better at reorgs—by providing them with a proven and practical five-step process for leading and implementing a reorg.

Who We Are and What This Book Is Based On

This book is based on over forty-five years of our combined experience as leaders of the organizational practice at the international management consultancy McKinsey & Company, as executives in business, as leaders of not-for-profit organizations, and as managers in the public sector. During this time, we have supported more than twenty-five reorganizations, big and small, and advised on hundreds more (some of their stories are included in this book as examples). The five-step process described here is our attempt to distill what we and our McKinsey colleagues have been practicing as an "art" into a "science" that executives everywhere can replicate.

As you might expect from two former McKinsey consultants, we have also grounded the book in analytical research, in particular a survey we first ran through the *McKinsey Quarterly* in 2010. This survey was based on responses from eighteen hundred executives whose companies had undergone a reorg in the past five years; from midlevel managers to the C-suite; from private firms to public bodies; across North America, Latin America, Europe, China, India, Asia Pacific, and the rest of the world; and covering business-to-business, consumer, energy, financial services, health care, high-tech and telecom, manufacturing, and professional services. Just over half of the results related to reorgs of the whole organization; the rest covered a particular function or business unit. The survey was rerun—with improvements—by McKinsey colleagues led by Aaron De Smet in 2014, covering twelve hundred respondents with a similar range of coverage.

In addition to our research and experience, we interviewed several prominent business leaders who have successfully led their companies through reorganizations. We will draw from those interviews throughout this book to illustrate the challenges of reorgs and how those leaders overcame them.

Why We Wrote It

When we started writing this book, several people asked us, "Why are you doing this?" The answer is pretty simple. This book is born of frustration: our frustration, as consultants who have been brought in to help companies through a reorganization; and, more importantly, the frustration of the people we've seen facing the challenge of a reorg. Over and over again, we have seen the debilitating consequences of bad reorganization processes that led to either poor designs or poor implementation (and sometimes both). Badly run reorgs cause massive human stress and cost shareholders value. Often, consultants like us are called in to help. More often than not, we are contacted midway through the process, when much of the damage has already been done. Conversely, external support is seldom sought when an organization is designing the detailed plumbing and wiring and planning phase of a reorg—which we see as the most challenging part.

It doesn't have to be that way. We always wished for a simple book or document that would help our clients move through the full process. Many books have been written on different organizational models or frameworks (the *answer*). But we struggled to find a book that laid out a simple, step-by-step way of doing reorgs (the *process*). So, we thought we'd better write one ourselves.

Avoiding the Typical Mistakes in a Reorg

The five-step process we present in this book should stop you from making two of the biggest mistakes in a reorg. Most reorgs start with the drawing of the organization design: what the boxes and lines on the new org chart are going to look like. And most reorgs end—or think that they have ended—when the new org chart has been announced. In reality, the process needs to start before you even envision the new org chart and must extend way beyond putting it in place. The five-step process therefore starts earlier and ends later than executives typically plan for.

This book gives you a ready-made plan and puts everything in the right order for you, at the right time. Through our experience, we have become firmly convinced that you need to have a plan so that you know what you are deviating from and what you must keep coming back to, as the various reorg brickbats are thrown at you. Having a set of steps to work through, in the right order, should help you avoid what happens all too often in reorgs: missing out on essential steps, the impact of which, as you will see, will only become apparent later, when it's often too late to fix them. Some practitioners advocate evolutionary change and making it up as you go along, because they can then be useful in leading you out of the chaos. Don't fall for this approach.

By contrast, the five-step process presented in this book gives you a clear menu for your reorg, extending from soup to nuts: it starts before you move around all the boxes and lines on the

FIGURE I-1

The five-step process

Content	Step 1: Construct the reorg's P&L	Step 2: Understand current weaknesses and strengths	Step 3: Choose from multiple options	Step 4: Get the plumbing and wiring right	Step 5: Launch, learn, and course-correct

Communications		Inform			Engage and excite
		Seek input			

Major reorg	• 1–2 weeks	• 3–4 weeks	• 4 weeks	• 6–12 weeks	• ~3–6 months
Minor reorg	• 1–2 days	• 1 week	• 1 week	• 2–4 weeks	• ~1–2 months

org chart and continues after the new organization is in place (figure I-1). As you will see throughout this book, there are many things that you need to remember if you want to get it right. You must do things in the right order to avoid delaying the overall process. For example, you need to set the business targets before you decide on new or adjusted job descriptions, and you need the job descriptions before you start staffing people into new roles. Similarly, you have to determine any required changes to your IT systems early in the process and conduct testing before you make the changes. If you do not, you can end up with a new organization without a profit-and-loss steering wheel.

What We Hope You'll Be Able to Do with This Book

Because our process works in practice and avoids missteps and rework, it should help you to deliver your reorganization much faster than the typical eighteen-month reorg. With this process, we've seen most reorgs happen in nine months or less—some as fast as three. At the same time, we don't pretend that reorgs are ever simple: we have lived through enough of them to know that they are not! But we are firmly convinced (by seeing the failings of reorgs that we have been brought in to fix) that the answer to this complexity is not to abandon all structure, treating the reorg as an evolutionary process and figuring it all out from first principles as you go along. This route typically leads to disaster.

In addition to a ready-made plan, the book provides checklists and templates for each step of the process. Appendix D contains blank versions of all the templates in the book. The templates are designed so that you can reproduce them and use them with your team, to organize and complete the tasks at each step of the process, in the right order and as quickly as possible. We hope that this book helps you navigate through the pitfalls that you will undoubtedly face and will help both you and your colleagues succeed.

Our approach works equally well in small businesses and large ones; in cross-business reorgs and individual business units and functions; and in reorgs run with consultants as well as those—probably the majority—run independently by company managers. We've written the book especially for those company managers. Even with smaller, simpler reorgs, the five-step thinking style is essential to keep you on track, although you may be able to complete a step in one afternoon for a simpler reorg, rather than spending weeks on it.

How the Chapters Work

We begin the book describing the findings from our research on reorgs. Our findings set the context for the five steps and explain why they work. We developed the five steps with colleagues in

McKinsey, basing the process on our experience and what the data told us.

Chapter 2 looks at engagement. Nothing seems to cause more problems than what executives communicate—and what they don't—during a reorg. Though there are specific messages to communicate, and ways to do that, at each step of the five-step process, it makes sense to address engagement all in one place, as it needs to run across the whole reorg. You will learn how communication needs to change over time and why, typically, one communications manager is responsible for leading the stakeholders' engagement.

After these two introductory chapters, we then devote a chapter to each of the five steps. Using stories and cases, each chapter describes one step, the typical pitfalls that managers run into, the "winning ways" to address the pitfalls, and how to manage communications. Each chapter concludes with a summary that contains tips that you can refer back to.

Where the Stories in This Book Come From

Reorganization is a contact sport, so the majority of this book is made up of stories, not analysis. We use a central story—of John, Amelia, and their global energy utility—as the backbone to the book. Each chapter begins with the pair falling into the common pitfalls of a reorg, and ends with an alternate version of their story where they avoid those pitfalls by using the process described in the book. The central story is based on a real case (with the challenges and subsequent solutions distilled into the two alternative versions of the story), but the names and industry have been changed to protect the innocent (and the guilty!).

In addition to the central case, we have used a number of anonymous cases that we have worked on over the past fifteen years to illustrate the winning ways of running a reorg, with the last ones in 2015. Although we did consider providing the company names, we wanted to share with you exactly how the reorganization actually took place. This information is never made public: companies only share the outcomes of their reorganizations (e.g., "We moved from seven regions to three!") but never how they got there or the problems they encountered along the way. For this reason, we had to draw on our own personal experience and contacts for the cases to make them real. Understandably, the companies concerned asked that we conceal their names, given the level of detail being shared.

As a reader of this book, you might be contemplating a reorganization to respond to the changing environment you are experiencing. You may be in the midst of the process, trying to get your organization back on the rails. Or you may realize that running a reorg is something you will have to do at least once in your career. We have written this book for CEOs who are reorganizing their companies, for senior executives who are leading the reorg or are affected by it, and for project managers and members of reorg teams. For this reason, you will see that our central case deliberately covers what happens from the perspectives of a CEO or senior executive (John) and a project manager (Amelia).

The Promise of This Book

We cannot promise to make reorganizations fun. You will be affecting leaders' powers and people's jobs. (If there is no impact on people, there's a good chance that little of significance is changing.)

Introduction

There will, therefore, always be difficult conversations. However, we can offer you an effective guide to negotiate your way through these conversations—a way to ensure that the results are worthwhile, to accelerate the process dramatically, and, most important of all, to minimize people's anxiety and treat them fairly.

"At last! The book I was looking for all the time!"

PART ONE

Why Reorgs
Are So Difficult

1

The Data

What Works and What Doesn't

As you might expect, as former McKinsey management consultants, we like to base our recommendations on the solid ground of data. This chapter draws on a survey we ran with the *McKinsey Quarterly* in 2010; the survey was repeated—with refinements—by colleagues in 2014.[1] The first investigation was based on responses from 1,800 executives whose companies who had undergone a reorg in the last five years. The respondents ranged from midlevel managers to C-suite executives; from private firms to public bodies; and spanned North America, Latin America, Europe, China, India, Asia Pacific, and the rest of the world. The industries included business-to-business, consumer, energy, financial, health care, high-tech, telecom, manufacturing, and professional services. Just over half of the results related to reorgs of the whole organization; the rest covered a particular function or business unit. The second survey in 2014 covered another 1,200 respondents with comparable backgrounds. The rest of this chapter describes what we found.

The Importance of a Solid Business Rationale

In this book, we argue that you should set and measure the specific *business* results of your reorg. But the fact is, few people do this. Our surveys show that only around 15 percent of executives set detailed business targets for their reorgs (such as specific P&L objectives) and only 37 percent set broad business objectives (e.g., an aspiration to grow revenues or reduce costs). Almost half set only qualitative targets around what the new organization might look like or how long it might take to complete. In analyzing the successes and failures of reorgs, we have, by necessity, sometimes had to rely on more qualitative assessments of each reorganization, although we have tried to ground this on any data that did exist (e.g., for a listed business, did the share price increase?).

According to our data, 70 percent of reorganizations deliver some value. However, only 16 percent of reorganizations deliver the results they are supposed to in the time they are supposed to (i.e., are an unqualified success). That means that over 80 percent of reorganizations fail to deliver their full objectives. Nearly half of executives say that their reorgs declared victory before the full changes were implemented. And, in 9 percent of cases, the reorg actually damaged the organization in the long run.

Stop for a moment to consider this. Imagine that you learned that less than 20 percent of your product launches, capital projects, or public sector initiatives had failed to deliver their full objectives, that almost 10 percent had actually damaged your business, and that the mass in the middle had limited or uncertain value. You would probably conclude that there is a significant scope for improvement. Later, we cover the reasons reorganizations have such poor results. But for now, it is important to realize that most reorgs are a failure (either relative or abject). So, if the approach we are advocating in this book contrasts with your experience of reorgs, do not be surprised.

Interestingly, the overall results differ remarkably little across type of business, industry, and geography. For example, the results for private and government organizations are almost identical (with only a few percentage points variation in each category of success and failure). By sector, energy and manufacturing achieve the highest number of unqualified successes, but even there, only 22 percent of reorgs deliver the results they are supposed to in the time they were supposed to. The data, of course, does not say why, but our guess is that the project management skills required in capital-intensive industries also work well in reorgs. The least successful sector in reorgs is consumer goods, with only 14 percent of reorgs delivering unqualified success. Across geographic locations, we see slightly more variation: in Latin America, 30 percent of reorgs experience total success; for North America, it is 19 percent; Europe, 11 percent; and Asia Pacific, 9 percent. So, as a rule, only around 10 to 30 percent of reorgs experience unqualified success, and 70 to 90 percent fall short in some significant way. Of course, it does not need to be that way: we can all learn from the success cases and raise the success rate. One obvious way is to reduce the number of reorgs that have no good rationale—which brings us to the reasons why leaders launch reorganizations.

Good and Bad Reasons for Reorgs

We appreciate that if you are reading this book, you have probably already decided to embark on a reorg and that, therefore, you might not be happy to learn that you could be doing it for the wrong reasons! That said, there are always things you can do to clarify the business objectives of your reorganization, as we describe in step 1, constructing a reorg's P&L (chapter 3).

Here is a good aphorism: your organization is perfectly designed to give you the business results that you have today. If you want to improve those business results, chances are you need to change an aspect of your organization: the structure (how you align people to deliver a particular set of objectives); the processes (how you go about doing this); or the people themselves (by redeploying them against different objectives, developing them, bringing in new talent, or reducing the number of activities, and hence people, if inefficiency has set in). Perhaps you need to do all three. But this seemingly obvious aphorism has a deeper truth: if you are not clear on the business results you want to change, you will not know where to change the organization, and you had better not start until you do.

Interestingly, the reasons why a leader launches a reorg have a significant bearing on its results. The reasons why companies launch reorgs will, of course, change over time: we see many more cost-cutting reorgs in down cycles and more growth-driven reorgs in up cycles. The McKinsey survey gives us a representative breakdown from the 2010s: facilitating growth (27 percent), cutting costs (12 percent), moving to a best-practice model (12 percent), bringing change into an organization that is too static (10 percent), reducing complexity (8 percent), fulfilling a new leader's desire to make changes (7 percent), responding to a crisis (6 percent), integrating a previous acquisition (6 percent), and facilitating a merger (6 percent), among others (6 percent).[2] With the number one reason, facilitating growth, the challenge is to maintain dynamism. As Elon Musk, CEO of Tesla and SpaceX, told us: "At first growth enables specialization and increases individual productivity. At about 1,000 people, overall productivity goes up but individual productivity falls . . . if you add too much structure and do not think about how information flows across the company."

That said, the survey suggests reorgs focused on delivering growth, and those to address complexity, are the most successful in the time frame planned.[3] Those least likely to succeed are reorgs intended to fulfill a leader's desire to make changes, to shake up an organization deemed too static, and to facilitate a merger. Reorgs driven by a leader's desire for change are also the most likely to lead to a negative impact on the business (21 percent of cases), followed by cost-cutting reorgs (18 percent) and mergers

(13 percent). This proves that reorgs need a clear business rationale to be successful, rather than one leader's desire to reshape the world in his or her image or a general feeling that things need to be shaken up. In addition, both cost-cutting reorgs and those linked to mergers and acquisitions (M&As) can be particularly tricky. For this reason, we devote detailed appendixes to both of these issues (appendixes A and B).

Compared with other reorgs, reorganizations designed to move to a best-practice model seem to do limited harm, but also add limited benefits. *Fortune* magazine found that the organizational designs of its Most Admired Companies had very little in common.[4] So beware when you hear that the next big thing is the [insert buzzword du jour] reorg, that you need to reorganize along these lines as soon as possible, and that you will then never need to reorganize again. Having a cool reorg concept is a great way to get people's attention, but the evidence does not suggest that it brings any benefits. Rather, you need your reorg to fit your company's particular strategy, culture, and capabilities.

Delivery Is as Important as Design

Responses to McKinsey's 2014 survey suggest that the success of a reorganization depends even more on how it is delivered than on why it is done. The survey also suggests that more reorgs go off the rails during detailed design and implementation than they do in the design of the original concept. Executives continue to declare victory after the concept design (which is often focused on the lines and boxes of the org chart alone) and take their foot off the pedal as they move into the more challenging phase of trying to get their people to work differently and deliver more value—the whole point of the thing. To avoid declaring victory too early, our five-step process covers every phase of a reorg; it does not end when the new org chart is created, as in most reorgs.

Given this context, it is probably not surprising that executives find it very hard to estimate the time it will take to reorganize. Only 37 percent meet the timelines they set themselves; 43 percent underestimate the time it ultimately takes; and only 20 percent overestimate the time needed. The average time to implement a new organization after coming up with the concept is twelve months, but 25 percent of reorg implementations take eighteen months or more, with some lasting years—we know of one reorg that has lasted twelve years! Describing her experience in one large organization, an executive who was on the team leading a reorg told us: "We are now two years into a process that should have been delivering at least a year ago. This has been horribly distracting for our organization, and we have spent far too much time trying to keep everyone happy when we should have just got on and implemented it."

Europe, in particular, takes longer to implement reorgs than do North America, China, India, and developing markets—not necessarily because of stronger regulations but more because of the failure to follow them properly. We therefore devote appendix C to the topic of European Union regulation for reorganizations and how to manage them effectively (a big problem for multinational companies). For some reason, Latin American reorgs take even longer (we would be interested to hear Latin American readers' thoughts on why).

The challenge of lengthy implementations is that they cause issues to be dropped and time to drag, prolonging the disruption to people and negative impact on business results and delaying the business improvements you wanted in the first place. The data shows that accelerated reorgs are much more likely to be successful. This contrasts with received wisdom that because reorgs are difficult, you should do them slowly to avoid upsetting anyone. But when you pause to think, the data makes sense. If you only get the results once the reorg is implemented, if staff will be distracted and upset during the reorg, and if business results will suffer as a result . . . well then, accelerated delivery of the reorg should be a no-brainer. With the process described in this book, we have seen many reorgs completed in nine months or faster. Smaller reorgs not affecting an entire enterprise have been completed in as little as three months. This is becoming all the more important, as companies need to respond to accelerated changes in the business environment.

Learn from Previous Reorgs

The fact is that reorgs experience common problems. But very few leaders stop to think much about this before launching their own reorg. Your own organization probably holds a wealth of details on previous reorgs—those that succeeded, those that failed, and those that landed somewhere in the middle. But this information typically resides in the collective memory rather than company databases. So, before embarking on your own reorg, ask around: What drove the difference between success and failure in your own company? And what other issues typically affect other reorgs in your sector? From our own research, we saw several issues that came up time and again. In frequency of occurrence, the challenges were the following:

1. Employees actively resist the changes.

2. Insufficient resources (people, hours, and money) are devoted to the effort.

3. Employees are distracted from their day-to-day activities, and individual productivity declines.

4. Leaders actively resist the changes.

5. The org chart changes, but the way people work stays the same.

6. Employees leave because of the reorg.

7. Unplanned activities (e.g., the unforeseen need to change IT systems or to communicate the changes in multiple languages) disrupt implementation.

These results are fairly common across business and geographical location, with a few interesting exceptions. Across almost all business sectors, the most serious issue is employees' active resistance to the changes. In the energy and financial sectors, by contrast, the biggest problem is that insufficient resources are devoted to the effort. So, if you are in one of these sectors in particular, make sure that you have correctly sized the scale of the effort required. In manufacturing, by contrast, the most common issue is that the reorg distracts employees and reduces productivity. Interestingly, implementation of a reorg is much more likely to take more than twelve months in manufacturing than in any other sector except health care, and individual productivity during reorgs falls further and longer in manufacturing than in any other sector. Similarly, in every region of the world except Latin America and India, the biggest problem is employees' active resistance to the changes. But in both Latin America and India, the biggest challenge by far is *leaders'* active resistance to change (with this issue causing serious problems in 42 and 33 percent of reorgs in these regions, respectively).

It should not surprise you that employees made miserable by reorgs may actively resist them. But surprisingly, resistance from leaders is also a major obstacle. After a little thought, the reason becomes clear. The organization that you have today is perfectly designed for its current leaders to succeed in. Change the organization, and you undermine their recipe for success and potentially take power and people away from them, too.

The half-life of upset morale is, however, limited. Around a half of the respondents told us that organizational morale was significantly hurt by the reorg in the short term, but that this figure fell below 30 percent six months after the reorg had been implemented. So, it is best to get the process over with as quickly and as fairly as you can, both for you and for your employees. Dragging out the pain causes more human misery, allows more time for resistance, and gives staff longer to dust off their CVs and find somewhere else to go. We have heard many people advocate for longer, evolutionary change when it comes to reorgs (often from leaders who want to postpone the changes until after they leave!). But a slower process just drags out the water torture. Good planning and speed are of the essence when it comes to reorgs. Again, this is an argument for acceleration.

It is possible to fully address some of the seven most frequent challenges to reorgs: you can devote sufficient resources, you can cover people and processes as well as changing the org chart, and you can get a better understanding of the activities you need to plan for (e.g., by reading this book). But with other issues, you can manage them better but cannot eliminate them: in particular, you can engage better with leaders and employees to minimize disruption, but you cannot make the disruption go away entirely. Reorgs that are completely successful (delivering their objectives in the planned time) still experience these issues, but about 10 percent less often. Many leaders believe that their reorg will be the first to avoid two common traps: first, that their secret plans don't leak out to the organization and second, that no one gets upset. If your reorg achieves this, it will be the first time we have heard of such a success! It's remotely possible, but don't count on it.

It Only Matters If It Matters to You

The surveys show that the senior leaders of the company or organizational unit undergoing a reorg spend almost one day a week on the reorganization. In a quarter of cases, leaders spend significantly more than 25 percent of their time on the reorg. India is the region where leaders spend the most time focusing on reorgs. And when a reorg involves leaders from the C-suite, they actually spend even more time on the reorg than when a reorg is run by more-junior business leaders. Interestingly, the energy sector—which has the highest proportion of successful reorgs—also sees leaders spending the most time on the topic.

Of course, spending time is not the only issue: leaders also need to be pulling in the same direction. The 2014 McKinsey survey revealed that in reorgs where respondents say their leaders were only slightly or not at all aligned on the reorg's objectives, just 1 percent were successful, compared with 49 percent of reorgs whose leaders were fully aligned.

The importance of senior leadership owning and driving a reorganization was something that many of our interviewees were keen to emphasize. Nancy McKinstry, who has experienced several reorganizations as a management consultant at Booz, then later as a business leader and the CEO of Wolters Kluwer, a global information services company, underscored this point:

> Most reorganizations are messy and involve breaking a lot of eggs. Many people do not realize quite how much energy they take up. You need to be sure that the size of the prize justifies the effort. Our last reorganization took up a third of my time over the first four months, and considerable time afterward. Leadership needs to have a burning commitment to the reorganization, or it will fail. So, don't start

one at the same time as your biggest-ever product launch! As a CEO, I get to see maybe four reorganizations over the course of my career. As a consultant, you see many more. That means there is a tendency to outsource the reorganization to consultants. You may need a consultant, especially at the beginning, to plan the process, but to be successful, you need to invest your own people's time—both people from the business and HR. That is what really makes the difference.

Neil Hayward, group people director of the UK Post Office, reflecting on his experience of running a major reorganization, agrees:

> If you imagine that there is another job that is more important than reorganizing your organization, then I don't know what you are doing. You cannot outsource it: you have to spend a lot of time on it, both individually and as a leadership team together. I made sure that we had a substantial executive team discussion of our changes every two weeks throughout the work.

. . .

So, what does all this sum up to? Have a good business rationale for your reorg. Focus on delivery as much as—or more than—the design itself. Recognize that there will be issues along the way; learn from previous reorg mistakes in your own organization and from the experience of others. Accelerate the process to minimize the upset for your colleagues and to deliver the business results you need as soon as possible. And finally, step up to the plate: lead your own reorg. Don't outsource to others. To help you prepare for this, the next chapter covers the typical issues of engaging with your colleagues and external stakeholders during your reorganization.

2

Communicating to Stakeholders

The Rules of Engagement

Befotre we talk about the five steps of reorganization, we will first look at engaging people during the reorg. Because engagement so often goes very badly, you should start to think about it right from the beginning, well ahead of any mass communication. It makes sense to talk about engagement as a whole: usually there is one person, a communications manager, who runs the process, and there needs to be a single plan, running like a thread throughout the whole reorg. In this chapter, we'll cover three elements of engagement: communicating with employees throughout the reorg; engaging with other stakeholders—unions, customers, suppliers, regulators, and the board; and preparing your reorg team to cope with the challenges of the process. Subsequent chapters will explain what to communicate, and how, at each step of the process.

Communicating with Employees

Leaders of reorgs typically fall into one of two traps when communicating with their employees. We'll call the first one *wait and see* and the second *ivory-tower idealism*. Perhaps you have seen one, or both, in your own reorgs.

In the first trap, wait and see, the leader of the reorg thinks everything should be kept secret until the last moment, when he or she has all the answers. The leader makes the reorg team and leadership swear to secrecy and then is surprised when the news leaks to the wider organization (it always does, we're afraid). As the reorg team starts to engage with the rest of the organization, the rumors round the water cooler increase: "They were asking what my team does"; "I had to fill in an activity analysis form"; "I hear that 20 percent of jobs are going to go." Everyone thinks the real reason for the reorg is job losses (whether it is or not). The leader, desperate to get in control of the situation, pushes the team to develop "the answer" so that he or she can tell the organization. Without an "answer," the leader feels that any communication would come across as defensive. At most, the executive approves some Q and A sessions on the reorg. But a full-scale communication needs to wait. Eventually, the leader has the answer: the reorg team produces a high-level org chart (we will find out later on why this is insufficient). The leader then announces the new organization: here are the new leaders, here is the structure, some job losses are necessary, but this is going to help us deliver fantastic results. Employees, hearing this, hear only that their boss's boss's boss is going to change and that some of them are going to lose their jobs. Nothing their leader has said counters the impressions they formed at the water cooler.

Ivory-tower idealism fares little better. In this version, the leader of the reorg is finally getting a long-achieved objective: all the issues of the old organization will finally get fixed; everything the leader wanted to do, but was held back from, can now be achieved. The leader can barely contain the excitement. So psyched up by the possibilities that the reorganization offers, the leader decides to start the process with a webcast to all staff, telling them about the exciting business opportunities it will open up. The leader follows this up with a series of walk-arounds in the major plants and offices, discussing the opportunities and getting input on some of the challenges that people face in the organization today. The leader puts a personal blog on the company intranet. Unfortunately, human nature being what it is, no one believes what they hear: they still assume the reorg is about job losses. The leader's enthusiasm for this change feels discordant to them. It sounds uncaring. Around the water coolers, the leader starts to become the object of ridicule. The enthusiasm of a charismatic boss becomes shipwrecked on a shore of cynicism. Until staff know what the reorg means for them—whether they have a job and, if so, what it is—they have no ears for the exciting future of the reorg.

So, how to handle this challenge? First, you do need to communicate often: much more than you would think is natural. Iain Conn, the CEO of Centrica and former CEO of BP's downstream segment, who has led three major reorgs, told us how important constant communication is:

> You need to treat people with respect and dignity, being transparent and telling them what is happening and when. You need to keep communicating with people. The biggest mistake is to communicate once and think you are done. You should keep communicating, even things people have heard already, to reinforce the message and ensure it sinks in. You should also never forget that you should be communicating to both employees whose jobs may be at risk and the vast number of employees who will stay with your company and make it successful.

Second, you need to be clear on what your staff need to hear from you. In both of the examples we gave above, the leader of the reorg is focused on the message he or she wants to get over to the employees. The communication is all one-way. If you instead focus on the needs of your employees, you would cover a very different set of questions: Why is this happening? What will happen when? What does it mean for me, my job, and my working environment? What do you expect me to do differently? One study has indicated that employees anxious about their jobs have significantly worse physical and mental health than do those in secure work: almost half experienced minor to major depression.[1]

You won't have all the answers to your employees' questions at the start, but you can minimize their anxiety by stating what you know now, what will come later, and when. Your task will be greatly simplified if you know why you are reorganizing and if you have an overall plan for the reorg (see chapter 3). In essence, communications should move from informing people at the beginning to exciting them when—and only when—they know what their new jobs are going to be. This is usually later in the process than the big announcement that leaders like to make when they have the concept design. Until they know whether they still have jobs, and what those jobs will be, staff have no interest in the fantastic strategies and metrics that make senior managers happy.

It is very important that staff hear their leaders talking regularly about the reorg, through internet sessions and town halls. You should continually communicate the one big thought of the reorg (e.g., move from print to digital, make local managers P&L accountable) and the three to five biggest organizational changes that will make this happen. For example, Elon Musk told us: "People at Tesla, SolarCity, and SpaceX feel that they are doing things that matter: if we can advance sustainable energy by ten years that is ten years less carbon." And with regard to communications, he added: "When companies get to be over a thousand people, and information has to flow from one person, to another person, to another person, you get a broken telephone . . . messages start to break down and get delayed . . . so I advocate for least path communication, not chain of command communication."

So, in addition to the usual approach of developing question and answer (Q and A) briefings and cascading information down through your managers, you should also encourage direct communications as much as possible. If someone has a question on the reorganization at any point in the process—and especially when the new organization is being rolled out—it should be clear whom in the reorg team or business area he or she should contact. Finally, you should ensure that there is a system for tracking whether communications are received and for capturing feedback that staff do not want to raise aloud: for example, you could provide a confidential e-mail address or regular web-based surveys during the reorg. The use of data to track communications—even the simple step of tracking whether anyone received or read the e-mails—is lamentable in reorgs. We know of one reorg where everyone thought the CEO's e-mails were going out to the whole organization. Three months into the process, they discovered that the e-mails were only being sent to senior leaders' e-mail boxes, where the messages remained, forwarded no further. Whenever communications are concerned, follow President Reagan's maxim: trust, but verify!

Some companies choose to go beyond simple communication and involve a cross-section of their staff in the actual design of their reorg from an early stage in the process. For example, in Thames Water, the UK's largest water utility covering London and much of the South East of England, Lawrence Gosden, the waste water director, engaged sixty members of staff from a cross-section of the organization, including the front line, in shaping the organizational design:

> We put them in a room with a lot of diagnostic material on the external challenges and some great facilitation, with the idea of stretching their thinking on how to address future

challenges. We then asked this group to develop a vision for what the new organization needed to do—including savings. The team came up with a simple vision focused on customer service. We then took the material and vision to our four thousand members of staff as a road show, in a way in which they too could explore what it meant to them. This generated an extraordinary level of ownership in the vision and reorganization to deliver it, despite the fact that some job losses were required.

Such openness from the beginning is a risk, and it won't work for every reorg. However, at the very latest, by the time that you start designing the detail of the new organization, you need to engage deeply with staff across the company, using their expertise to get the plumbing and wiring right. You can't design all the detail with a small team of smart folks in a room. And when the new organization launches, it will be the employees who determine whether it will deliver value: will they work in the new way you expect, or will they continue as before but with a different boss (or a different boss's boss's boss)?

Communicating with Other Stakeholders

Most executives running a reorg end up creating a communications plan for employees, even if this is typically done late in the day and significantly underestimates how much communication is required. Far fewer leaders spend significant time thinking about other stakeholders. In the communications sections at the end of every chapter, we too will also focus mainly on staff within the organization as the most important focus of communications. Depending on your particular business context, however, there are up to four groups of people whom you also need to cover in your engagement plan.

The first group is the unions and workforce councils. In the European Union, legislation requires you to communicate with representatives of the workforce at a fairly early stage (see appendix C for details). If you don't do this, you can screw up your reorg, often making life harder for workers outside the EU who may have to bear the brunt of higher savings. In Asia, unions can also be very important: they may be linked to governments, parties, and other power blocs. Perhaps surprisingly, unions often have some clear views of what needs to be changed and can sometimes be even tougher than management (e.g., "Why don't we just remove the middle layers of management?")—although their focus is usually on employees who are not their members. We always recommend at least speaking with unions, not only to tick a legal-requirement box, but also to get their ideas. On a few occasions, we have even had union representatives as members of a reorg team.

The second group is your customers and suppliers. The danger of a reorg is that it can lead to navel gazing. If your business is customer driven or relies heavily on the supply chain, you must ensure that the new organization works better for these stakeholders than the old one did. Laying out the steps in a *customer journey* or the full value chain of your business, including suppliers, is a great way to ensure that interactions are simpler and more effective in your new organization than they were in the old. (It is also an argument for focusing on the processes of your organization as much as, or more than, you do on the org chart.) It is a good idea to interview particularly trusted or representative customers and suppliers to get their views on what needs to change as an input into your reorg. In the case of business-to-business customers, you should equip your sales force with a simple set of Q and As in case customers hear about and ask questions on the reorg process.

Again, it is very difficult to keep the reorg a secret from them if (as you would hope) your salespeople are also friends with your B2B customers.

The third group is regulators and other arms of government. This group is typically very risk averse and will want to know that the reorg will not affect quality, health, safety, and other outputs that they care about. Briefing regulators and other government actors at a senior level on what is going to happen, when it will happen, and what it means is the first step in reassurance. As with customers and suppliers, you will also need to check that in the new organization, you have designed a simple, effective way of engaging with this group. Avoid at all costs the situation in the following real-life story. The country head of the Asian arm of an international company was meeting with a senior government official just after the reorg. The official asked him for an update on the company's performance in this country, as he had done many times before. "Oh no," the manager responded. "This isn't my responsibility anymore. You need to speak to our new operations excellence team in the United States." Remember: regulators and government officials—like customers—don't want to have to negotiate the complexities of your internal organization. So, make life easy for them.

The fourth group is the board of directors. If your reorg is companywide or is likely to have a major impact on company performance, it will be of interest to the board. You don't make an omelet without breaking eggs, and reorgs always lead to some short-term penalties. It is critical, therefore, that the board understands what you are doing, why you are doing it, the time frame, the risks along the way, and the benefits that will result. At the very least, the CEO, or other leader in charge, should brief the board members individually and collectively on the progress of the reorg, just before the end of each step outlined in this book. You may also want to engage them in choosing the answer or at least in defining the principles or a solution space that they are comfortable with. Lord John Browne, the former CEO of BP, who has also served on the board of Goldman Sachs and in the UK civil service, has this advice for executives: "The board have to be involved in the design. You should advise them that the path may be rough, but that they should ignore the bumps in the road. The board needs to understand the design and what you are forecasting the outcome will be. You need to set out simple milestones and report back on them on whether you are delivering against these."

Preparing Your Reorg Team

Let's now consider the type of challenges a reorg practitioner might encounter. Throughout our combined twenty-five years of supporting reorgs, we have experienced plenty of interesting actions. We've had a client try to punch one of us, and another client snap our computer screen in half when he prodded it too vigorously in his disagreement. We've seen clients and colleagues burst into tears and meetings terminate abruptly when managers were too angry to continue. A director of a company once threatened to throw one of us in a river, and one of the carefully chosen leaders of the new organization walked out immediately on being offered the job. One of our former colleagues had a manager pull a gun on him and tell him, "You are not taking any of my people—not a single one!" In another instance, a consulting team was photographed by the local union, and the photo was put on a billboard outside the HQ, with the headline: "These are the people responsible for getting rid of your jobs." These things are never easy (although, hopefully, your experiences will never reach these extremes).

Your reorg team—likely a project manager, an HR representative, a finance person, a communications specialist, representatives from the organizational units affected, and perhaps a union official—will need to be able to cope with difficult situations. An executive running a reorg will make a great start by picking the right kind of people (robust, analytical, fair-minded, grounded in the day-to-day business, and personable) in the first place. Access to senior management support to break through roadblocks will also help. And, as the process moves on to more-detailed design, you are also likely to need business unit or functional unit design teams. Finally, a solid understanding of the process they need to follow (e.g., by reading this book) will help the team members navigate through the storms and avoid being blown off course.

Armed with a good understanding of the data (what works and what doesn't) and the needs of your workforce and other stakeholders, along with the right—well-prepared—reorg team, you are now ready to take the first step.

PART TWO

A Better Way

The Five-Step Process

3

Step 1

Construct the Reorg's Profit and Loss

"Aha, there are the benefits . . ."

F irst, a quiz for you. For your current reorganization, or one you have been involved with before, what answer would you give to the following questions?

How precisely did you define the value the reorganization was supposed to bring?

0: No value defined; reorg simply seen as a good thing to do.

1: Some ideas about where value would come from (e.g., better sales productivity), but not quantified.

2: Overall value target set for the reorganization (e.g., reduce head-count cost by 10 percent), but not broken into specifics.

3: Value precisely defined and quantified (e.g., $x million cost savings and $y million increase in sales revenues).

To what extent did you consider the costs and risks of the reorganization?

0: We assumed that we could deliver the reorganization without any costs or disruption.

1: We identified some high-level risks (e.g., staff disruption, exit of key people) to help plan mitigations.

2: We created a budget for the project team or external support and identified some high-level risks.

3: We created a budget for the project team or external support and quantified the potential risks of the reorg (e.g., 5 percent decline in sales during the period of uncertainty).

How did you judge the timeline for delivering the reorganization?

0: No timeline set; it takes as long as it takes.

1: We set a timeline for the first phase of the work (e.g., drawing the new lines and boxes).

2: We set an overall timeline (e.g., the reorg must be complete by April).

3: We set an overall timeline, broken down into the phases of the work.

Add up your scores for each question. What score did you get? If you scored 7 or more, then you are doing pretty well: you are clear on why your reorganization is happening and what it will take, and you have a timetable in place. A score of 4 to 6 means you have some of the basics in place. Below that, and you are in serious trouble. We hope that this chapter helps you recognize the gaps in your program and do something about it. Without clarity on these questions up front, how can leaders even know if a reorganization has been successful or not?

To better understand the challenges that reorgs face, we introduce you to our central case (where we have anonymized the characters and changed the industry).

John has just become the CEO of an energy utility company straddling the United States and Western Europe, with recent investments in Eastern Europe and Asia. The company was originally established in Europe. John is the first CEO from the United States and is relocating with his family to Europe, to live near the company's HQ. He is excited about the chance to improve performance and wants to mark the start of his new role with a dramatic act. From his previous position as head of the US business, John concludes that the company is deeply inefficient. It is ill prepared to navigate growing environmental worries, consumer choices, price pressure, and regulatory change. He believes that the firm is currently less than the sum of its parts. Several local businesses have been bolted together, with limited sharing of approaches across them, and the corporate HQ sits on top, adding cost but little clear benefit. With the current structure, his scope for improvement seems limited. He becomes convinced that what is required is a root-and-branch reorganization. He will have plenty of other things on his plate in his first hundred days. So, he turns to a trusted employee, Amelia, who worked with him on a previous business issue in the United States.

Amelia was excited to get the phone call from John, who advised her of her next challenge. He had briefed her in broad terms. But since then, she has been struggling to meet with the new CEO in person to understand the challenge in more depth. John has been traveling around the world, meeting the board, investors, and his new leadership team. In the meantime, having found little help in the available literature, Amelia goes back to first principles. As she comes from a capital-projects background (her last job was managing the construction of new onshore wind farms in Texas), Amelia decides to use the stages in a capital project as an analogy for the reorg: first, understand the opportunity; then develop the scope, choose the concept, detail the design, and deliver; and, finally, run the new organization.

Starting at the beginning, she concludes that there must be a concrete business objective for the reorganization.

Two weeks after the first phone call from John, Amelia is finally able to speak to John by telephone. She shares her thinking on the reorg. John likes her approach. "But let me take some time to share my thoughts on the reorg," he adds. "Look, I figure that the way we are set up today, it just gets in the way of doing what we need to do. Take capital projects. All that good work you did with the wind-farm projects. That has no influence on how we are approaching renewables in Europe. Those guys are just reinventing the wheel. Then, let's take a look at the folks in HQ. We have so many people working in the center, asking for information from each of the businesses. This creates a hell of a lot of work. But the businesses never hear where that information goes, what gets done with it. And next time around, there is a whole different template to fill in. As I compare our company with our competitors, they have 10 percent lower costs than we do. I hate to say it, but we have too many people, too much inefficiency. And with the traders, it feels like we are still approaching everything from an engineering perspective. If we compare ourselves with the banks—and I know those guys don't always get things right, either—we are in the dark ages. And again, each country seems to have its own process for doing this. My vision is that we have one central organization, one single system, that can deliver a trading platform across all our country businesses, done in the best way. So many of these issues come down to how we organize. Without a reorg, I see little chance of delivering the results I've promised to the board."

"I'm also concerned about safety performance across the company," Amelia says. "We have really driven some improvements in the United States. But if I look at the performance in some of our other business units, especially in emerging markets, the injury statistics are very worrying. It is only time before we have a fatality. We need to get this right for the company and for the people who work for us—whether they are staff or contractors."

"I very much agree," John replies. "I know this is all new to you, but I've got a lot of faith in your abilities, given the improvements you delivered in the North American business. I'd like it if you could also move to Europe—for the time being at least. You can have the office around the corner from mine. It's going to make it easier to work together on this. Now, I know I've got a lot of other things to do. But I want you to get time in my diary at the beginning and end of every week. Work with my assistant, Richard, to get this booked in. I'd also like you to interview my direct reports. Find out what they think we need to do. And put together a team of people to help you on this. Whatever you need to get this done, let me know. I want the reorg put in place, at least for my reports and their reports—let's call it the 'new operating model'—by Christmas latest." (It is now August.)

Amelia follows John's suggestion to interview the top team of country CEOs and functional heads. Again, it takes time to get the meetings and phone calls set up—partly because the European leaders are on summer vacations. Some calls take until September to set up, the CEO's urgency notwithstanding. The leaders are split fifty-fifty in their opinions: one side agrees with John's assessment; the other, while recognizing external problems faced by the business, sees the current organization as working well. This second group accepts that they need to make some changes to fit in with the CEO's ideas. But it's obvious they would prefer that the changes are minimal.

In mid-September, Amelia creates a project charter based on her discussions with John and his team (figure 3-1). This charter helps, but Amelia still feels that there is insufficient clarity on what the reorg is supposed to deliver. Some of the company's

FIGURE 3-1

First draft of a reorganization project charter

Objective	
• Reorganize the company	

Benefits	Decision makers
• 10% cost savings in head count • Best-in-class capital efficiency • World-class trading performance	• CEO

Costs	Stakeholders
• Project team: ~$300k for 3 months • External support?	• Country market-unit managing directors • Heads of functions in corporate center (HR, finance, trading, capital projects)

Risks	Sources of information
• Leadership misaligned	• Experts in the market units and functions

Scope and timeline	
• Top three layers of the organization structure • 3 months (phase 1)	

leaders, particularly those in the corporate center, see the change as a turning point in the company's history. Others, particularly in the country market units, see it as an incremental change, building on the company does already.

At least the cost-reduction target is clear: a 10 percent reduction in the cost of people. However, this does not specify if every part of the organization should have the same cost reductions or not. Even from her short visits and interviews with business units, it's clear to Amelia that each one has a different starting point. Some business units have achieved significant cost savings already; in others, a simple walk around their head office and a look at the cars in the parking lot (their makes and numbers) reveal that efficiency is not a priority. Also worrying is that some leaders see the 10 percent as a stretch target rather than a commitment. Finally, even if these reductions can be found, Amelia is already worried about how she is going to handle conversations with her colleagues, some of whom are friends, about job losses that could affect them.

Beyond cost reductions, the other objectives are less clear. What do "best-in-class capital efficiency" and "world-class trading performance" mean in practice? Amelia is new to senior management discussions and worries that she might be seen as not getting it if she raises these kinds of questions. Hopefully, it will become clear, she thinks to herself.

Although John told Amelia that she can have "whatever she needs," the line organization is reluctant to free up experts from the different market units and functions. It does not take her long—through the input of friends and colleagues in the different bits of the business—to work out which thoughtful, experienced people she would need. But the business unit leaders seem reluctant to free up these people full-time ("the people you're asking for come out of my budget; you can have them full-time if you put them on your own payroll!"). For now, these experts are still focused on their local businesses, mostly doing their day jobs. In practice, they are only joining a weekly call and adding comments. Amelia feels that she is doing all the work and then having her homework marked by others. Maybe it would be better to get some external help? But how much would this cost?

But on one part of the process, Amelia feels more confident: the discussions with John and his leadership team have at least settled the timeline of the project. Within three months, before she and her colleagues break for Christmas, she needs to deliver the *operating model design*, which means the top three layers of the company's reporting structure: the CEO, the market unit and corporate leaders, and the leaders of their teams below. At that point, the project will be handed over to HR and other experts in the organization. This timeline means that, by Christmas, Amelia should be able to return to her day job.

By using her intuition and natural intelligence, Amelia is doing better than most leaders at this stage in a reorganization. However, she is right to be worried. John has identified a few areas where his company could perform better, but he has not articulated a clear rationale for why a reorg is required and how it will help his company compete in the market.

Iain Conn, the CEO of Centrica and the former CEO of BP's downstream business, shared his view on the secret of effective reorgs: "You must know, with real clarity, what you want the organization to be and stand for, ensure that the goals you set are realistic, and reorganize to deliver that. For our recent reorganization, we spent twenty full working days meeting as a top team over the course of six months, understanding what we do today, the markets in which we operate, where those markets are going, and what our strengths are." This clarity should cover the benefits that the reorg should deliver, the costs and risks of the reorg, and the time frame for delivering. It's critical that you focus on the future—on where your market is going and how your company should compete in it—not on fighting the battles of the past.

By contrast, John and Amelia are falling into three of the most common pitfalls of step 1.

Pitfall 1: Ill-Defined Benefits

As in the case of many cost-focused reorganizations, Amelia at least has a high-level target for cost reduction. A reduction of 10 to 20 percent is, of course, the usual target, and, as usual, Amelia's target focuses solely on employee head count. But what about the costs associated with head count (like procurement, office costs, travel, and expenses)? What about the cost savings from reducing contractor spending (which often goes up when head count goes down)? What about the savings, or increased revenues, from better managing the business? And what if some parts of the organization need increased spending on head count to deliver these results, whereas others (such as pet projects launched by previous leaders) can be cut by 90 to 100 percent? The blanket 10 percent cost-reduction target does not enable Amelia to negotiate these sensitivities and set differentiated targets. It also means that every conversation she will have with a business leader will be yet another battle or horse trade. Worse still, she does not have a way to hold the conversations about trade-offs with her leadership group. She has regular access to the CEO (although we will later show that other pressures get in the way of this), but so far, there is no forum for decision making across the leadership group—no way to address her nagging doubt that not all leaders are on the bus.

Now, a word on the use of benchmarking costs and head counts as a way to set targets: beware. We have experienced both high-level benchmarking (e.g., so many HR professionals per employee) and detailed, activity-driven benchmarking (e.g., the number of finance staff in accounts payable per invoice processed). Based on this experience, we have developed some firm views on benchmarking. We have grown skeptical about the use of detailed, anonymous benchmarking: it encourages a "rush to the bottom" when, in reality, the lowest number of staff does not guarantee the best performance or even the lowest cost (given differences in locations and salary). Benchmarking is also very difficult to calibrate between companies, which may make very different insourcing and outsourcing decisions, affecting the numbers significantly. In addition, few companies consider forward momentum when setting cost-reduction targets: if one business unit is growing rapidly, while another is stagnating, it does not make sense to hand out 20 percent cost-reduction targets to both, whatever the benchmarking says. Maybe the growing unit should get 10 percent—to ensure that the growth is not stunted—and the other should get a 30 percent reduction, given the more serious financial situation. Sadly, the blanket 10 to 20 percent haircut is the more common approach, whereas setting differentiated targets, according to a variety of business inputs and management judgment, is much less common. This one-size-fits-all approach is appealing probably because a fixed rule—however wrong—is much easier to stand behind in the emotionally charged context of a reorg, whereas a more nuanced approach, which by definition involved a management judgment, focuses attention on the person who made that judgment. Although it's difficult, our advice is to be brave: it will be better for your business and fairer for your colleagues.

We have seen cost benchmarking work well in two ways. The first is internal benchmarking: the approach across one company is typically quite similar, and where it is not, you at least have the ability to find out how and why it is different. So, it can be helpful to ask, why do I have twice as many HR staff per employee in Europe than in North America? One obvious explanation for the difference in this example might be the need to speak different languages in the European department. However, with this great of a difference, there are probably some efficiencies to be had. The second form of benchmarking is shared benchmarking between a small handful of companies. When companies can share data and openly compare the differences, it's possible to have a rich discussion to understand where the opportunities are on all sides. For example, we arranged a discussion between a global oil and gas company and one of its leading suppliers to compare their approach to HR: not only the overall people numbers, but also the approach to supporting business needs and the location of that support.

In Amelia's case, interpreting the cost target has its problems, but at least it has a number. The challenge with what we might call the *effectiveness* targets is their vagueness. While reorgs are often associated with reducing costs (as this is a simple thing to do), it is equally—and sometimes even more—important to also consider how they can increase revenues. Even with the most cost-focused reorgs, it is helpful to find at least one major way of improving effectiveness too: no sense in saving the company now, only for it to fall apart, with no way of winning against the competition afterward. Alastair Swift, CEO of Willis Transport, told us about one reorg he was involved in: "We were trying to do a lot of things in one go, and the focus moved quickly from a growth agenda to a cost agenda and rationalizing our operating income. There was a palpable shift of management attention to the easier, executable cost reduction versus the tougher thing to look at—revenue growth." For companies running reorganizations whose primary purpose is not cost reduction (it could be, for example, growth or managing risk more effectively), any vagueness around these benefits will be even more significant.

In Amelia's case, we need to ask, What is capital efficiency? Does it simply mean spending less capital, building each wind farm or gas-fired power plant cheaper than the last one, or maximizing the returns on capital spending? And what does world-class trading performance mean? Given that you don't get what you don't measure, how are things measured? These are examples of the "motherhood and apple pie" statements that often get used in reorgs—that is, statements that everyone would agree with, but that imply no choice or specific action to achieve them. To avoid such statements in your own reorganization, you can apply the following test: if you reverse the statement, is it so ludicrous that no one would ever argue for it? If so, then you have motherhood and apple pie. Consider: "We want to have worst-in-class capital efficiency" or "We want poor trading performance." No one would ever argue for these things. Yet, a statement such as "We want 10 percent capital efficiency" could be reversed and still make sense. We might not want 10 percent efficiency, because 5 percent, 20 percent, or 30 percent is in fact the right answer (of course, we still need to define what capital efficiency actually is, or, again, we will not be sure if we actually achieved it).

At the same time, companies need to avoid entrusting the solution of every problem they have ever had to the reorg. Lawrence Gosden, the director of wastewater services at the UK's biggest water utility, Thames Water, has experienced a number of reorgs. He told us about the importance of having a specific purpose for a reorg:

> Getting the purpose of the reorganization right is critical.
> Usually, you end up with a dirty list of everything, and at
> some point in the reorganization, you realize that there are
> many things you are never going to deliver. You need to be
> ruthless and focus on the top few things that really matter.
> Ultimately, these need to link very clearly to a few numbers
> that count for shareholders, customers, or both. As a part
> of this, you need to be prepared to deprioritize other areas,
> which are still important, but where you are prepared for
> performance to be just OK—or even, on occasion, not quite
> good enough—in the interests of delivering great perfor-
> mance in the areas that matter most.

Pitfall 2: No Consideration of Resources Required (Financial and Human)

Amelia is trying to get clarity on one aspect of the resources required: the makeup of the reorganization team. This is critical. Lord Browne, the former CEO of BP, recommends that executives consider three things before launching a reorg:

> First, find a dozen allies who understand the purpose of what you're doing, but more importantly the tone and behavior that you want at the end of your reorg. Remember that you are changing interactions as well as structure. Without those, don't even try. Second, set up a reorg project team under one of your trusted allies, whereby you have someone who can help subdivide the problem and task people to set out a micro plan for each division. Third, remember that as a CEO it's easy to lay down performance criteria, but different to get people to change behavior.

Typically, a reorg project team would include a project manager (like Amelia), an HR representative, a finance representative, a communications expert, experts on each part of the organization that will be subject to change, and—depending on context—a trade union representative. In addition, as two of our interviewees pointed out in the introduction, leaders need to commit their personal time to leading the change, or it will not be effective. Of course, these commitments vary with the size of the reorganization (they could be part-time roles or roles combined across a few people). But they require real work and tangible responsibilities. Occasional attendance to mark someone else's homework is not sufficient. The cost of this input can quite easily be calculated if one knows the time commitments and rough pay bands. As a rule of thumb, table 3-1 shows the levels of effort and the indicative costs for different reorganizations.

Next, as Amelia identified, is the cost of any external consulting support. As we noted, this may not be required at all if there is internal expertise and if the change is relatively simple. But outsiders may well be required if the value of the reorg is high, the solution unclear, and the change highly political (in which case having a neutral party involved in some of the discussions could help you reach agreement). Again, this element should be easy to cost, as any such support should have an accompanying, costed proposal from the third party (but be wary if this proposal is only for some of the five steps outlined here when in fact you need help across all of them).

TABLE 3-1

Resources needed and approximate costs for different types of reorganizations

Type of reorganization	Resources	Cost*
Part of a business unit or function	1 full-time project manager: 20% HR, 10% finance, 10% communications, 10% leadership time	$180,000 for 9 months
Whole business unit or function, or small company	1 full-time project manager, 1 full-time expert on business unit or function: 50% HR, 20% finance, 20% communications, 20% leadership time	$250,000 for 9 months
Whole company (midsize)	1 full-time project manager, 8 half-time experts for each function or business unit: 50% HR, 20% finance, 20% communications, 8 x 20% leadership time	$1.25 million for 9 months
Whole company (very large)	1 full-time manager, 1 full-time support, 10 full-time experts per function or business unit, 1 full-time HR: 50% finance, 50% communications, 8 x 20% leadership time	$2.15 million for 9 months

* These are not out-of-pocket expenses but enhanced labor costs of employees who work on the reorg.

A Better Way

Finally, the costs that Amelia did not consider—and which are rarely considered—are the human costs. Like many others before you, you may believe that yours will be the first reorganization to avoid the human cost of a reorg. Unfortunately, you will be wrong. More than half of eighteen hundred executives that we surveyed saw a significant dip in productivity, a 10 percent slippage in deadlines, or a 10 percent drop in sales—or some combination of these difficulties—during the reorganization.[1] This slippage is significant and far outweighs the costs of project team or consultants. Of course, there are steps you can take to mitigate some of these risks (such as retention bonuses and an accelerated tempo of management reporting, so you can identify issues early and intervene to help your people— not to beat them up), but these steps also come with their own financial costs.

Even if you are able to mitigate the human cost, you cannot remove all of it. All reorgs result in changes to roles even if the number of roles does not change. And some reorgs will substantially reduce the number of roles and people. All of this leads to employee stress, which has to be considered before you start the work. You need to be sure that the benefit you are creating for shareholders, customers, or the health of the organization more generally outweighs the human cost of the change, including the cost to individuals. And you have to be prepared to tell people who have worked with your company for a long time—who may indeed be friends—that their jobs have substantially changed or have disappeared entirely. So avoiding this pitfall does not mean removing the human cost—you cannot remove it. Instead it means calculating a realistic set of internal and external costs and being sure that the benefits justify both the financial and the human costs involved.

While you cannot remove the human cost of a reorganization, you can reduce it, and throughout this book, we highlight ways of doing that. Here are the most important things to do:

- Communicate as much as you can as early as you can, including timetables for when decisions will be made.

- Treat all employees with the compassion you would expect yourself, and anticipate that people will respond to the reorganization emotionally. This means setting aside substantial leadership time to support employees affected by the changes. (The affected employees are not just those who are leaving the organization.)

- Test the changes thoroughly before implementing them, and make sure they are understandable at a role level, not just at the level of a CEO or senior manager. Each employee needs to understand how his or her role will change on the first day of the new organization and needs to have the skills and motivation to make that change.

Pitfall 3: No Agreed-On Timeline

Amelia feels that she at least has clarity on her personal timeline for the reorganization and the deliverable she needs to produce ("the top three layers of the company's reporting structure"). However, when seen from the perspective of the reorganization as a whole, this timeline is incomplete, first, because the timeline only goes to the end of the concept-design phase (step 3) and, second, because the definition of her deliverable is itself incomplete (as we will see in chapter 5). We firmly believe that the endpoint of a reorg should not be the creation of a pretty picture of the organization's lines and boxes, or the detailing of what this concept means, or the launch of the new organization; the endpoint should be when the new organization starts to deliver more value. This is how you would judge a business project. Of course, this is hard to do if that value is ill defined. Amelia will find this out the hard way as, inevitably, her project is extended through and beyond Christmas (lucky her!).

Because the typical approach to reorganizations can best be described as "one thing after another" or "let's make it up as we go along," and because most managers have limited experience running a reorg (especially a good one), we seldom see an agreed-on timeline for the full reorganization. Or if we do, it is usually much longer than it needs to be. As a consequence, most reorganizations take around eighteen months to complete. Since the average tenure of a *Fortune* 500 CEO is less than five years, eighteen months is a significant time commitment. Indeed, in the twelve-year case we referred to in the introduction, only the third CEO finally managed to declare victory and close the reorganization project. However, not only had this project by then consumed a huge amount of management time and attention, it had also, over the years, gradually been amended to satisfy different executives so the result was a highly inconsistent design across divisions, functions, and locations. In our experience, successful reorganizations are much more likely to be completed quicker: in three to nine months. From the perspective of minimizing the disruption to your employees, it should also be obvious that the quicker you get a reorg done, the less human stress it causes. While this should be a commonsense conclusion, many executives running a reorg fall for the line that long, drawn-out, evolutionary change will minimize disruption. Please do not make the same mistake.

. . .

So, benefits, costs, timeline—what does all this sum up to? If we know these three variables, we can understand the P&L of the reorganization (see figure 3-2 for a conceptual illustration of this through the life cyle of a reorg). More than this, we can question at the beginning whether the reorganization is worth doing at all. If the numbers do not stack up, then the answer is obvious: do not reorganize. Even if they do stack up, you should still ask: "Can I accomplish my objectives through other, less disruptive, means that would reduce the human cost?" If the answer is yes, then you should not reorganize.

Unfortunately for Amelia, the leaders of her company have not had this conversation and understand only the purpose of

FIGURE 3-2

Conceptual illustration of a reorg P&L

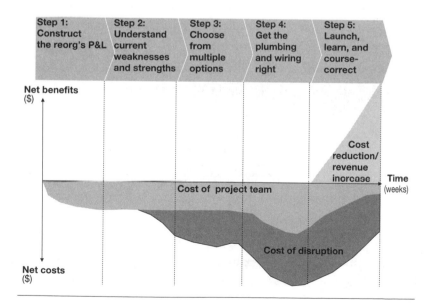

the reorg at a theoretical level (it is a turning point, or it is an incremental change). Given the challenges ahead, these phrases are unlikely to convince people to change. Executives who have been through a reorg process have underlined this point to us. For example, Hannah Meadley-Roberts, the director of the president's office at the European Bank of Reconstruction and Development, told us: "The most important thing to have before you start is a really compelling reason for the change. Even if the reason is negative, such as a need to cut costs, if it is clear, then everyone can be galvanized to get on with the change." So our advice is that you should only do a reorganization if you have the rationale clear, that it is agreed on across your executive team, and that they understand the cost of the change. If this has not happened, stop.

Of course, you may hear two objections to this approach (we certainly have): First, some argue that reorganization is a people issue, not a business one, and should therefore be seen as an enabler to business, not something you can measure in itself. The second objection is that reorganization is a complicated business with lots of variables, which means that you can never precisely define the value. If you have read up to this point, you can probably guess our opinion on this first point: it takes us back into the realm of pseudoscience. If the reorganization is necessary to deliver the value you want, you should certainly be able to measure whether you achieve that value. We absolutely agree that a reorg, like almost any business project (such as expansion into a new geographic region), is a people issue. But you would never dream of embarking on any other project without clarity on its purpose, so why do it for something with such a high human and financial cost? If the reorg is not necessary, and there are less costly, less time-consuming, and less painful ways to realize this value, you should probably not reorganize at all.

With regard to the second point—that you cannot precisely define the value at stake—businesses make these kind of estimates about complex initiatives all the time. For example, the oil and gas industry decides whether to invest in multibillion-dollar capital projects when they have only drilled a few wells, do not fully understand the quantity and quality of the reservoir, and certainly do not know what the oil price will be in ten years' time when the project has been built (goodness knows what it is as you are reading right now). If they can do that, then we can certainly estimate the benefits, costs, and timeline of a reorg.

We will now take each of the three challenges (around benefits, costs, and timeline) one by one, and, using cases from our experience, point to winning ways of dealing with them.

Winning Way 1: Explicitly Define Value

Our experience with a European courier company illustrates the importance of explicitly defining the value of reorganization. This company wanted to establish a corporate university to replace its diverse range of training courses and had created a business case to support its plans. The project team, led by the HR director, saw the main benefit of the university as cost reduction, by delivering all the courses together in a more efficient way. However, the business case was marginal, and when line leaders resisted the idea in the executive committee discussions, the CFO reluctantly supported them and rejected the plan.

After this unpromising start, the project manager forced himself to return to the drawing board. He realized that he and his team had been approaching the value of the university from the wrong angle. There was some benefit from cost savings. However, two other sources promised to deliver much greater benefits. The first was refocusing the resources already spent on training away from generalist training and toward specific capabilities that were needed to deliver the business plan (like cross-selling). And the second was making the organization more attractive to employees—which would both make it easier to hire staff and increase retention. In both cases clear business targets were set and tracked through to the bottom line.

The project manager realized that he had been lucky to have the first business case rejected, as a corporate university set up to deliver new skills and greater employee stickiness would need to be set up very differently from one focused on cost reduction. To deliver the shift in the focus of the training, the corporate university would need to have the right to recommend training priorities to the executive team (rather than just letting the current set of courses continue but in a more efficient way). To improve the attractiveness of jobs, the university would need to be closely aligned within HR and have solid links to the recruitment and retention functions.

Winning Way 2: Identify Risks as Well as Costs

The head of M&As at a major mining company was considering a big acquisition. He was aware that the biggest thing that could go wrong, after the purchase, was for the integration of the two companies (one form of a reorganization) to take too long, cost too much, or—worse—fail to deliver the business results the company needed (see appendix B). He therefore devoted his energies not only to laying out the full timeline (right through to delivering the expected cost reductions and putting in place new processes across all mines) and costs (both internal and external), but also in detailing the risks to delivery.

Almost one hundred risks were identified in total, ranging from talent loss to business disruption to delays in bringing in new managers. However, across these one hundred, he then identified twelve that, if not addressed quickly, could create bottlenecks in the integration process. For example, a delay in deciding on the pay grade structure for the merged company was identified as a bottleneck risk, because until this was decided, jobs could not be advertised. Such bottlenecks were very closely monitored through the integration, and when the timing on any of them slipped (as inevitably some did), the leadership team immediately intervened (better planning does not mean you won't have challenges). While other decisions were monitored, intervention was less urgent when timetables changed.

This approach of identifying bottleneck risks is one that we have regularly used in reorganizations to ensure focus and rapid intervention on the decisions that will prevent progress. Incidentally, bottleneck risks are not always the biggest risks—they are just those that could substantially delay the overall reorg process.

Winning Way 3: Set an Accelerated Timeline

An international industrial company was in dire straits. When global recession struck, the industry entered a serious downturn, and demand dropped. The company needed to save over 10 percent of its costs in less than six months simply to survive. This could not be achieved by incremental tinkering: the company required a full-scale reorganization to respond to market changes. At the same time, the leaders of the company were painfully aware that getting this reduction wrong could accelerate the company's demise.

The CEO of the business decided to take dramatic action, announcing to the market the savings target and the timing of the reorg. From then on, there was no debate around the timeline: the company simply had to deliver. To achieve its goal, it avoided overcomplex planning and instead set a few crystal-clear deadlines. It charged fifty of its top talent with the job of managing the transition, developed a detailed cookbook to help local businesses implement the changes, and developed a people-mapping tool to track the savings in people costs.

The company succeeded in reorganizing even faster than it had hoped, in just four months. This change was very painful, as many employees needed to leave the company, but the clarity of the objectives—and the consequences of not meeting them—meant that the employees involved were treated like adults. Moreover, a clear process for making decisions ensured that the reorg was done as fairly and sensitively as possible. Operations in a few European countries that were heavily regulated and unionized took longer to make the transition, but they were not allowed to hold up the wider effort (see appendix C).

In addition to achieving its cost-reduction targets, the CEO and his team were painfully aware that they not only needed to shed costs to survive, but also had to create a leaner way of operating that would enable them to succeed when the upturn came. Despite the accelerated timeline, the company still made time to test a new logistics IT system before it was rolled out.

Because of these efforts, the company achieved its cost-saving targets and continued to grow and improve performance despite a difficult market.

. . .

What does all this mean for Amelia and her reorganization of the energy utility? Let's imagine that she had the advice contained in this chapter. What might she do differently?

Through her conversations with John's direct reports, Amelia realizes that some of the leaders are buying into the program, whereas others are just pretending to play along. In her weekly conversation with John, she therefore makes the following suggestion: "Rather than continuing with one-on-one conversations, how about we have a couple of workshops, as we would do to make a major capital project decision? In the first one, we can get together with a few of the leaders who are most enthusiastic about the reorg. We can agree on the benefits of the reorganization, its risks, and its timeline. In the second workshop, we can bring together the full leadership team of the company, including the country market unit heads and corporate HQ leaders. They can see how important this is to you, and we can address the issues together. There will be no place to hide. And, John, I really need your help to free up the team members I need and get them posted here to HQ."

"Sure, whatever this takes," he says.

"One more thing," she says. "Er . . . capital efficiency and world-class trading performance. I'm afraid I don't know what these really mean . . . I mean, how we might measure them."

"Right. Me neither. Let's talk about them in the workshop."

Before the first meeting, Amelia, now helped by her team, pulls together some facts that will help her, John, and their closest allies create a first version of differentiated cost-reduction targets for the organization. Her team looks at the financial comparisons with the company's competitors and compares each of the businesses with each other: for example, why are there twice as many HR professionals in one business unit than another? At the same time, the team members try their best to understand the performance of the business units, too. It turns out that one country has slightly more financial controllers than the others, but also has the best control of costs. They make a note not to assume that staff members necessarily deliver the best performance. They also put together options for measuring capital efficiency and trading performance. On health and safety, all parts of the organization are obligated to monitor injuries in the same way, but only the most serious injuries are reported to HQ. With the CEO's authority, Amelia gets hold of the full set of numbers, which increases her alarm that, in some regions, a major incident is only a matter of time away.

The forthcoming workshop with the leadership team forces Amelia's team to raise its game. No one wants to look stupid in front of the leaders of the company. The leadership team reviews their work. Amelia points out that people savings alone will not deliver the targets, and she shares the results that indicate that the lowest number of people does not always deliver the right outcome. John and his trusted advisers realize that the operational expenditure (opex) savings need to be delivered through a combination of staff savings and reductions in other spending (such as outlays for contractors, materials, and services). The group works through each of the market units: some, with more challenging economics, are given much higher savings targets; others (such as the capital projects team) are allocated increased investment to build the capabilities necessary to drive down the costs of construction. An increased revenue target is set for the trading business. And the team clarifies that capital efficiency means building future capital projects 10 percent cheaper than the previous ones. Interestingly, the capital-efficiency target is bigger than many of the main opex savings, even though operational expenditures generate much more controversy.

On Amelia's suggestion, targets are also set for safety performance. Without wanting to seem too callous, the team finds that it can also calculate a monetary value on safety, using recent insurance payments, regulatory payments, and project delays. John and his team are surprised to see that this makes safety one of the most important business targets, as well as a moral duty in itself.

The team next addresses the potential costs and risks of the reorganization. Before the meeting, Amelia completed some analysis on the performance dip during the company's last reorganization. She noted almost a 5 percent drop in billing collections, asset utilization, and trading performance and hypothesizes that the distraction of employees was the cause. These potential drawbacks are then set against the benefits of the reorganization. The economics still make sense, and John is reassured that Amelia already has some ideas to mitigate the potential risks.

The group sets a timeline of nine months for the full reorganization, basing the number on the need to start demonstrating financial impact in the second half of the next year and the lengthy, eighteen-month duration of the previous company reorganization (widely seen as being poorly managed). The case for this accelerated timeline is clear to everyone in the room: the benefits will arrive earlier, and the disruption will be shorter. However, it also means that significant senior leadership time will be required through those nine months, particularly toward the end, when the human impact of the change is being managed. Given the appreciation of the longer time scale, Amelia deliberately plans around holidays—her Christmas is saved. Now the challenge is to deliver the reorg.

Finally, Amelia lays out the time commitment and the costs of her project team. She also includes the requirements of senior management time. After having shown the potential benefits and costs of the reorganization, Amelia finds the discussion much simpler than she had expected. The CEO signs off on the full project team and promises to intervene again if the business does not continue to support with resources.

The second meeting, with the full leadership team, proves much more challenging. Given the difficulties of getting senior management time, Amelia plans it for the day before the regular quarterly management meeting, so that as many leaders as possible can be there in person. Even so, some country market unit leaders are unable to attend. Based on what she knows about their opinions, Amelia suspects that their nonattendance may have been deliberate. On Amelia's suggestion, John opens the meeting: "Let me take some time to share my thoughts on the reorg. I figure that the way we are set up today, it just gets in the way of doing what we need to do." John tells them that the overall targets are non-negotiable; he and the board have already agreed on them. The team's job today is to review the breakdown of these targets into country market units and functions.

Amelia then leads the discussion on the opex targets. It is a tough conversation with the market unit heads who face the largest targets, arguing for why they should be given more freedom. It is helpful that John gets to see some of the resistance himself. At the same time, some of the feedback is useful. For example, Amelia learns that some improvements planned for capital projects can be achieved without investment. At the end of the meeting, there have been a few adjustments to the targets for individual market units and functions, but the overall target remains the same. While the leadership team would not have originally voted for this outcome, the team accepts that the changes are necessary and that the process for agreeing on the targets was fair.

In addition, the executive team discusses the likely human impact of the transition, including the need for each team member to commit time personally to support members of staff who will be affected by the change. John makes clear that all the team leaders need to set aside time each week to communicate with their people on this.

On a personal level, Amelia is pleased that her passion for improving safety has become one of the main targets of the reorganization and that there has been an explicit discussion about the change's impact on people. On the basis of her two meetings, Amelia now updates her project charter (figure 3-3) (for changes to the scope—people, process, and structure—see chapter 5). After only a few weeks, Amelia feels much more comfortable about what she needs to deliver.

FIGURE 3-3

Second draft of a project charter

Objective
- Reduce costs and increase revenues through a companywide reorganization

Benefits	**Decision makers**
• 10% overall cost reduction in opex (with individual targets for each unit): $100 million annually • Higher trading revenues: $50 million in 2 years • 10% capex savings per project: $30 million annually • 90% reduction in lost time through injury in 2 years	• Decision committee, chaired by CEO, including representatives of country market units and central functions

Costs	**Stakeholders**
• Project team: ~$600k for 9 months • Leadership time: $650k for 9 months • External support: $500k budgeted	• Country market-unit managing directors • Heads of functions in corporate center (HR, finance, trading, capital projects) • Workforce

Risks	**Sources of information**
• Decrease in collections: ~$20 million one-off • Decrease in asset utilization: ~$10 million one-off • Decrease in trading revenues: ~$2.5 million one-off	• Historical reorganization experience • Experts in the market units and functions • External support

Scope and timeline
- Organization people, process, and structure
- 9 months (implemented and starting to deliver value)

How to Handle Communications in Step 1

The first principle of communications in a reorg—as with anything else—is to start with the needs of your audience. It is a simple, commonsense piece of advice, but one frequently forgotten, as the leaders focus instead on what they want to communicate to their people.

- **Staff and leadership needs:** This is the one step where, potentially, you can get away with keeping relatively quiet while a small team investigates the business rationale for launching a reorganization or not. But do remember that the more people who know that a reorganization is being considered, the more likely the news is to leak. If, at the end of step 1, you do decide to go ahead and form a full reorg team, the staff will want to know what is going on and will fear the impact on their jobs. Leaders, who may know more about the plans than other employees know, will probably be even more concerned about changes to their roles, their power base, and any future progression. At the same time, both groups will have other concerns in life, will probably know that the work will take a while, and will not expect immediate changes.

- **What to communicate:** At this stage, you do not know exactly what the reorg will look like, but you do know the business rationale and—as we strongly argue above—you should have a plan for what happens when. This is not the time to try to excite anyone with the coolness of your early organizational ideas. Instead, communicate simple facts: the broad business reason for the reorganization, which areas will change and which will not, the milestones by which leaders and staff will know more about the reorg. If your reorg is in the European Union, be careful about the language that you use at this stage and whether it implies that certain decisions have already been made (see appendix C). It can also be beneficial to announce the people you have selected for your reorg team. If the team members are well respected in the business, your selection of them will send a message to the organization that the reorg is being treated seriously. If there will be no layoffs, say this (but people will probably still not believe you). If there are, or may be, layoffs, do not rule them out, or you risk credibility later. For leaders, identify the top talent that you cannot afford to lose; approach them and assure them that they have a place in the future organization. At this stage, many leaders worry about whether they should make a big announcement regarding the reorganization. The benefit of such an announcement is that when you associate it with a positive business objective, people can more easily follow the story of the reorganization over time. However, an announcement has the disadvantage of making the reorg seem like a very big deal, which can make people more worried if the communications are not well handled.

- **How to communicate:** Communications at this stage should be very simple, perhaps an e-mail from the CEO and a notice in a personal blog (or equivalent) if the CEO has one, with a focus on the process being followed, not what the reorg might look like. Ideally, a two-way form of communication should be set up for questions (e.g., a dedicated e-mail address), although the team should not be obliged to share any details of the reorganization until they are ready to be more broadly communicated. In addition to aligning communications with the decisions made in each step, it can be useful to set the expectation that there will be regular updates during the process (e.g., in the CEO's blog or with a monthly conference call). Regular communication avoids a vacuum and lets people know when they can expect to hear news. And when the news does come, it arrives with the feeling of "Here is the latest in our monthly updates" rather than "News flash! I have an announcement to make!," which either can feel alarming or, if there is actually little to say, can seem disappointing.

Step 1 Summary

Pitfalls

- Benefits ill defined

- No consideration of resources required

- No agreed-on timeline

Winning Ways

- Explicitly define value

- Identify costs and risks

- Set accelerated timeline

How to Use These Ideas in Your Organization

- Question whether the reorganization is worth doing at all: are the benefits worth the costs (including the human cost) and risks? Use the P&L template found in appendix D, like the one in this chapter.

- Create an end-to-end plan for the reorganization, starting with defining the P&L (benefits, costs, risks, and timeline) and describing how leaders will know that the reorg has realized those benefits. You should expect your reorg to take longer if the organization is bigger, if you plan to bring in a lot of external talent to fill roles, or if you operate in countries with more complex legel requirements.

- Set up a project team, including a project manager, an HR representative, a finance representative, a communications expert, and an expert from each of the organizational units that will be affected (depending on the scale of the reorganization, some of these will be part-time or combined positions, but they need to involve real work).

- Ensure that leadership commits time to leading the change:

  – Hold a first meeting between the project sponsor, advisers, and the project team to define the reorganization's P&L.

  – Hold at least one (potentially several) meeting with the leadership of the organization to get its input. This is not a democracy (few people would vote for reorganizations), but the voice of leadership needs to be heard now: it cannot be circumvented. Otherwise, you will later have to face the arguments in one-on-one battles.

  – Agree now on the likely time required from the leadership to support the change, and be careful not to underestimate the time needed in the later stages, when leaders will be needed to counsel and support affected employees.

- Capture the overall objective, benefits, costs, risks, timeline, scope, decision makers, stakeholders, and sources of information in a project charter like the one in figure 3-3, using the template in appendix D, and share among the team.

- Make a wider announcement to the organization, focused on what is happening, why, how long it will take, and when they will hear more.

4

Step 2

Understand Current
Weaknesses and Strengths

A gain, we'll start this chapter with a quiz. Please answer the questions on your current reorg, or a past one, before moving ahead to design a new one.

To what degree did you evaluate the strengths and weaknesses of the previous reorganization?

0: We did not do this. The previous reorg did not give us what we wanted, so it was clear we needed a new reorg.

1: We conducted some high-level benchmarking to compare the previous reorg with other options (e.g., pros and cons).

2: We investigated the weaknesses of the previous reorg to help us know what to fix.

3: We investigated the weaknesses and strengths of the previous reorg in detail. We therefore knew what not to break.

Whose views did you consider for this evaluation?

0: No one's; we did not consult others' views.

1: Leaders of the company or business unit or function.

2: A cross-section of staff, namely, 10 to 20 people drawn from leaders, experts, and frontline workers.

3: A sizable sample of people (100 to 200 people) drawn from different levels and regions (perhaps even including some customers or other external stakeholders).

How did you conduct this evaluation?

0: We did not do the evaluation.

1: Interviews only.

2: Interviews and surveys.

3: Interviews, surveys, workshops, and analysis (e.g., activity analysis, analysis of financial or operational metrics, comparisons of good and bad performers).

Again, sum up your score. You should feel pleased with a score of 7 to 9 and concerned with a score below 5. What does the result say about the degree to which you know (or knew) the patient you are (were) about to operate on? Would you be happy if your personal surgeon had conducted this level of due diligence before reaching for the anesthetic and the knife?

Now, let's see how your experience compares with Amelia's.

Amelia has the clarity she needs on the reorganization's objectives. What's next? Well, she knows that what the CEO, John, really wants is the design of the top three layers of the new organization (its "operating model"). Once this has been done, she and her team can complete their mission, hand everything over to HR, and move on. But Amelia feels intuitively that it is first important to understand the way the organization is organized today so that she can specify what will change. She therefore asks the experts in each business to send her the existing org structure charts and any other relevant information, such as how their market unit allocates capital or makes trading decisions. She creates a shared drive for the full team so that everyone can have access. This will be helpful when the detailed design starts later.

Amelia realizes that it is important to understand which bits of the organization are particularly challenged today. She creates an interview guide for each market unit and corporate function to ensure that she identifies all the most relevant issues—whether they relate to strategy, capital projects, trading, commercial activities, customer relations, operations and maintenance, or back-office support. She then interviews each member of the executive team to understand which issues need particular attention. Country heads complain of an overbearing corporate center where the functions try to impose too many decisions, whereas functional leaders complain of significant variability in the way each country unit works and, ultimately, performs. On some issues, however, the leaders agree: there is excess cost in the business (although each leader points to another part of the organization as the biggest problem); the process for capital projects is unclear; and capabilities in the trading organization are severely lacking. The US business, in particular, believes that it has already addressed many of these issues (especially reducing head count) and that the main problem is Europe's failure to keep up.

Amelia synthesizes her findings in a short presentation and shares it with John, the CEO. He is very impressed by her work, reassured that many of the worries that he himself feels are shared by his team, and glad that other issues he has missed have been highlighted by her interviews.

How would you rate Amelia's achievement for this step? From our perspective, she has done as well as could possibly be expected for someone who has not run a reorganization before. In fact—as we will see below—many reorganizations skip this step entirely. Nonetheless, she has again fallen into three dangerous pitfalls.

Pitfall 1: Focusing Only on Weaknesses

In a reorg, it's very tempting to have the mind-set of wanting to fix the organization. In this frame of mind, it is natural for us to focus only on the negatives. But pause for a moment. How much of the organization is actually broken? Remember the aphorism "your organization is perfectly designed to deliver the business results you have today." Are these results completely unsatisfactory, or only in some areas? The results of step 1 will give you the answer to this question. If all your business results are appalling, perhaps you should only focus on the weaknesses and assume that everything will need to change. If, as is far more likely, some results are good, some bad, and some just OK, then you should also ensure that you spot the strengths, highlight them in your communication to the organization, and make sure you do nothing that upsets them. In most reorgs that we have seen, only 20 to 30 percent of the organization actually changes. The trick is to identify the right 20 to 30 percent. Beware of starting at the top and trying to change everything, only to see the effort peter out before reaching the layer responsible for the real business outputs.

Consider a medical analogy: A surgeon is planning an operation on a cancer patient. She starts with a diagnostic, where she attempts to delineate the diseased tissue from the healthy. Now, she may remove a small amount of healthy tissue as a margin, to make sure she gets all the bad. But she will do all that she can to avoid unnecessarily cutting into healthy tissue, lest she cause unnecessary damage to the patient.

Executives running reorganizations are seldom so careful. Even in cases where strengths are clear, companies can find that one of these strengths disappears when their new organization is launched.

For example, one energy client found that when it changed its organization to drive standardization and efficiency, its previous strength of strong P&L ownership disappeared. Top-down reorganizations run this risk more than surgical, bottom-up ones (more on these two approaches in the next chapter). It is therefore as important to spend as much time in this diagnostic phase identifying the organization's current strengths and working out how to preserve them as it is to delineate its weaknesses.

You also need to use this diagnostic to understand the capabilities of your leadership and staff. Their capabilities—in particular their ability to handle change—will shape how much your organization can change. In fact, during this step, some executives running reorgs decide that they will need to hire one or more new leaders from a competitor or another industry—someone who has experience with the new capabilities that they want to develop and who can help them lead the changes they need.

Pitfall 2: Listening Only to Leaders

Amelia focused her diagnostic efforts on interviews with the company's leaders. This makes sense. Leaders run the business. Only they have the strategic view of what is important and what is not. But what else is a leader? Leaders are also human beings, defined by their own desires and experiences. They may perceive some parts of the organization as weak, simply because the parts do not fit with the leaders' personal objectives or those of their business units. This is nothing unexpected: it's a natural phenomenon and, often, a part of strong ownership mentality. However, it means that you also need to corroborate and challenge their views by securing objective facts and by asking others.

Leaders also typically see the problems of the present through the prism of their past experiences. An operational leader who has moved up through the line organization cannot help but understand problems in terms of his or her own frontline experience. Again, this is part of a leader's strength. However, the world may have changed since then. Today's generation has very different skills, attitudes, and expectations. Regulation may have moved on. Competitors behave differently. New approaches have been invented. Or a leader's formative years may have been spent in one particular region (say, Asia) and now the leader is running the US business, which will have some similar, but also many different, challenges. A leader may know this intellectually but is often still emotionally influenced by the biases of his or her early experience.

All this means that in a diagnostic, you need to reach the parts that others cannot reach to understand the issues from different perspectives. This means going down through middle management (the "clay layer," as we often term it, because of its intransigence) right to the front line. And it means understanding the regional differences if a company has a large geographic footprint. Neil Hayward, group people director of the UK Post Office, told us how he went about this step: "I was shocked how little was understood centrally about the organization before the work began. You need to understand not only which roles sit where but also what those roles do. When we did this, we discovered that we had to remove a largely redundant layer in the organization that in most divisions was not really required."

From our experience, we have found that three things hold true across many companies. First, leadership is usually more optimistic than the front line. Next, leadership and the front line often agree on many solutions, but the sticking point is middle management, which often has much less incentive to change. Finally, the United States and Asia are usually more optimistic than Europe. Of course, these trends are sometimes overturned, and when they are, we have an interesting case on our hands, where we really need to dig deeper.

By searching for the positives within a company, you may also find solutions to problems. Suppose we are working in a consumer goods company and the sales function is not working well. We want to fix it. But rather than implanting an idea from another company—an operation that risks organ rejection—we might find that the sales function in one business unit is doing better than those in the others. From this successful unit, we can learn an approach that actually works in the rest of the company. (In Amelia's case, it is worth investigating whether the US business unit really has solved many of the issues or if it is simply being more optimistic—as our experience might suggest.) We might even move some of the staff from this successful business unit to others to pollinate good practices. That would be a far better idea than imposing an approach from another company that we don't fully understand.

Talking to the whole organization (or a sample of the whole organization) is often not enough. Ideally, you need to go further in your diagnosis and understand what people outside your organization think. John Ferraro, the former COO of EY, advises leaders running reorganizations to "look beyond the boundaries of the current problem. Really look at what stakeholders want. Be willing to be radical." To do this, we encourage our clients to seek the views of customers, suppliers, and other stakeholders to understand what these groups would like to see from the company or business unit.

Pitfall 3: Relying on Hearsay

Amelia has done her best to put together a fact base for the reor-ganization, but so far all she really has is hearsay: what the lead-ers of the company have told her they believe. Of course, this is in itself a fact: leaders really do feel this way (although it is also not uncommon for them to reveal a partial picture to influence events). But it is not sufficient. You also need to get some more objective facts on the table. One set of facts are those from step 1: facts about the performance gaps in the company. Comparing these and what people say enables you to perform a very sim-ple analysis, which we like to call "what leaders think is broken" (from the interviews) versus "what really matters" (from the analy-sis). If you do this, you can then construct a Venn diagram like the one in figure 4-1, which we have populated with examples taken from Amelia's case.

FIGURE 4-1

Venn diagram of what is broken and what matters

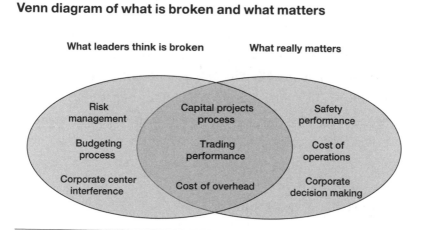

This is a helpful analysis, because it can guide your actions. The category that is shown in the intersection between "what leaders think is broken" and "what really matters" is the sweet spot. The second category, things that "really matter" but that no leaders seems to think are "broken," is harder: they are potential blind spots for leadership. You need to think through the argument for change more carefully. The third category, things that leaders think are "broken" but that don't really matter, is the one to be careful of. It can suck in a lot of time and effort, with very little benefit. You might launch a few actions in this area simply to gain support for the reorg. However, you should clarify early on (in fact, in this very step) that this category will not be a focus for the work.

It is also important to understand the reasons behind the gaps in performance, particularly if one objective of the reorganization is cost reduction. First, you need to define the costs that can be influenced through the reorganization, that is, internal staff costs, contractor costs, related costs where the number of staff is the main factor (e.g., travel, expenses, and computer costs), and other costs that are influenced by staff numbers, but that may also have a fixed-cost element (e.g., buildings and training). The critical thing to understand is the *activity drivers* of these costs and how they can be addressed. For example, in the compensation and benefits function of HR, you might look at the number of compensation benchmarking studies carried out and understand whether you can run them less frequently, more efficiently, or both. Unless you understand how these activity drivers can be reduced, you will find that contractor and/or head-count costs will start to creep up again later (for further details, see appendix A).

To do this, you need to tap the wisdom of the organization in a structured way, through surveys. This task goes hand in hand with the previous points we made about reaching deeper into the organization. If you are working with consultants, they may have an existing structured survey you can use. If you are working alone, there are simple ways of developing your own survey by listing all the elements of the organization (across process, people, and structure), printing each element on a "playing card" and having interviewees sort these cards into separate piles on a "game board" (e.g., "significant issue," "not an issue," and "strength"). This approach, which we have used many times, enables interviewees to sort through dozens of issues in a short period of time when discussion of all these issues would take hours. It enables you to quantify the results of the interviews: Do people agree on the issues or do they disagree? Are there any interesting splits—for example, between corporate center interviewees and business leaders? And it is a more fun and interactive way of engaging with interviewees. Table 4-1 illustrates organizational issues for a corporate center reorg, figure 4-2 illustrates an issue card, and figure 4-3 shows a game board. Social media—such as company discussion boards—are another great way to gather insight. One objection we often hear about this approach is that it will spread alarm in the organization. However, you will be kidding yourself if you think that people know nothing of your plans. And typically, asking people what they think is a great way of building support for your actions (as long as you then listen to their feedback).

Having considered these three pitfalls, let's now look at some real-life examples of winning ways to address them.

TABLE 4-1

Sample organizational issues for a corporate center reorg

People

1. Alignment on future strategy

2. Clarity around the role of the corporate center

3. Time and effort focused on the decisions that really matter

4. Alignment among the management team

5. Appropriate balance between timely decision making and consensus

6. Appropriate balance between common central decision making and local responsiveness

7. Constructive challenge to decision making

8. Analytical rigor informing decision making

9. Establishment and communication of a corporate vision

10. Direction provided to the business by the corporate center

11. Desired culture driven by the corporate center

12. Desired behaviors determined and modeled by the corporate center

13. Strategy capabilities

14. Planning capabilities

15. HR capabilities

16. Finance and accounting capabilities

17. Commercial capabilities

18. Analytical capabilities (e.g., network modeling, forecasting)

19. Capabilities in operations

20. Capabilities in capital projects

21. Contracting and procurement capabilities

22. Government relations and other stakeholder management capabilities

23. Regulatory capabilities

24. Customer management capabilities

25. Risk management capabilities

Organizational structure

26. Organizational structure to support development and implementation of group strategy services for the business

27. Organizational structure to deliver HR activities

28. Organizational structure to deliver finance activities

29. Organizational structure to support contracting and procurement

30. Organizational structure to deliver secretarial function

31. Organizational structure to handle external relations

32. Organizational structure to handle regulatory engagement

33. Organizational structure to deliver transactional services for the business

34. Clarity on division of accountability between corporate center and the business

35. Clarity on division of accountability within the management team

36. Shared services provided to the business by the corporate center

37. Centers of excellence established in the corporate center

38. Location of corporate center activities

39. Risks identified in the business by the corporate center

40. Size and capability available in the corporate center

Processes

41. Strategy development process

42. Initiative prioritization and business planning

43. Investment prioritization and approval process

44. Capital project delivery process

45. Contracting and procurement process

46. Talent attraction and development process

47. Employee engagement

48. Safety process

49. Finance process

50. Risk management process

51. Performance measurement and management process

52. Standard setting and assurance process

FIGURE 4-2

Issue card

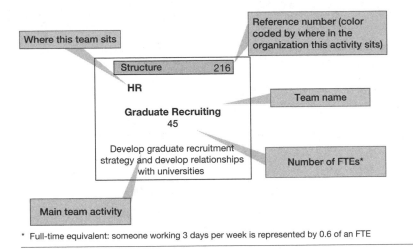

* Full-time equivalent: someone working 3 days per week is represented by 0.6 of an FTE

FIGURE 4-3

Game board

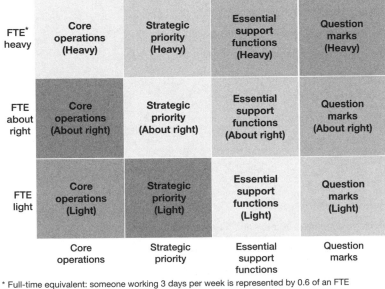

* Full-time equivalent: someone working 3 days per week is represented by 0.6 of an FTE

Winning Way 1: Identify Strengths to Preserve

An Asian oil and gas company was entering challenging times. It had recently received a large investment from an international partner. But despite years of success, both the original owners and the international partner were disappointed by the company's current performance. It was clear that planning, exploration, and capital project design needed to improve. A project manager was appointed by the international investor to discover the root causes of the current problems—and to identify the causes of the company's historic success.

Compounding the project manager's problems was a cultural dimension: given the Asian company's kudos and the oversupply of highly qualified professionals in the local market, employees were unwilling to speak up about what was really going on, for fear of losing their jobs. This reticence was both to their own detriment (they lacked empowerment and felt disenchanted) and a problem for the company's leaders (when no one tells them what is really going on, and when no one else is willing to make decisions, leaders have to work very hard). This cultural challenge made it difficult to understand the root causes of the organization's weaknesses.

At the same time, seconded staff from the international investor also came with their own cultural baggage. Many of them could only see the weaknesses in the Asian company. They thought that if only Western practices were substituted for the company's own, all would be well. They failed to appreciate the company's strengths. In fact, in terms of speed of decision making, innovation, contractor cost management, and speed of project delivery, the Asian company had a lot to teach its international partner.

The project manager sought our help in getting beneath the two cultures and finding out what was really going on. For the Asian company, we used a mixture of surveys and one-on-one interviews with a cross-section of staff. While these staff were not happy to speak out in public gatherings, in the one-on-one sessions, with the promise of confidentiality, they were very open about both the weaknesses and the strengths of the company. The weaknesses were a lack of collaboration across different functions, a lack of formal processes to judge risk, and insufficient delegation (as the company expanded its operations, it was no longer practical for all the decisions to be taken by top leaders). At the same time, we also learned the strengths of the company: the ability of its top leaders to make decisions quickly and whenever required (versus the more bureaucratic approach in international companies), how quickly work was delivered in response to these decisions (the speed outstripped international peers), and the quality of the technical staff working in the company. Rather than presenting this in a typical PowerPoint deck, we instead printed out posters containing the research, data, and the interview quotes (covering issues that had been raised by multiple interviewees). Senior leaders of the Asian company and the international investor viewed the posters in a gallery, taking their time to digest what they meant, given that this was the first time they were hearing any of these inputs.

Given the importance of maintaining a company's strengths, we knew that the trick in designing the new organization would be to identify the capabilities that the Asian company could source from its international partner to address its weaknesses, without undermining its strengths. This approach would mean modifying dramatically any processes that we imported into the company to make sure they would work in the very different culture into which they were being implanted.

Winning Way 2: Make Sure You Hear Everyone's View

One of our projects was with a consumer goods company that, historically, had performed very well and had a long track record of creating highly innovative products. However, in recent years its innovation had faltered while that of its competitors had risen. The leadership team was very conscious that sales were decreasing but could not understand why organizational performance was declining, why decisions were taking longer to make, and why less interesting new products were being suggested to senior management.

We started our work with a broad survey of the organization to uncover the most important issues. Unlike the typical executive overoptimism that we mentioned above, the leadership in this company was far more negative than middle management or the front line. As we looked into this further, conducting a series of interviews at different levels and mapping some of the processes to see how they were broken, we found that the leaders were more negative because they had a much better perspective of how the company was placed relative to competitors—and knew the answer was not good!

The survey gave us a clear indication of what was going wrong. A huge amount of work was being replicated across the different levels of the organization, with the regional structures duplicating much of the work carried out at country level, and the global organization triplicating it. This was hugely frustrating to everyone in the organization and meant that decision making was very slow. The duplication of effort was not the only issue—for example, there were also problems of performance management, with very little being done to address low performance in the business, meaning employees lacked the motivation to do an excellent job—but it was the primary one.

The business could have addressed this problem through changes to processes so that staff clearly knew who was responsible for each step. The challenge was that this was likely to be a temporary fix; with so many people in the structure having overlapping responsibilities, the processes would become complicated again after a while. So we advised a more radical fix: abolish regions almost completely, which would give countries far more autonomy and speed up decision making. Though this change was hard to implement, it created much more fulfilling roles across the structure, as managers were much more empowered and there was therefore much less second-guessing. We then redesigned the major processes (like product innovation) to simplify them and to reflect this new structure. Together, these changes shortened product innovation from fourteen months to six.

Winning Way 3: Triangulate with Analysis

In another example, working with a very fast-growing Asian retailer, we again conducted a survey to figure out where the company was working effectively and where it was doing so less well. This company had grown its revenues by more than 200 percent per year by rolling out retail franchises across different countries. However, it suddenly found that its impressive growth had stalled. Our analysis showed that the number of decisions had grown and grown as more and more franchise brands had been added, until the whole decision-making process, which had originally been very informal (almost all decisions were signed off by the CEO or CFO), had become logjammed like traffic on a highway. Executives were hugely frustrated as decisions that used to get made in a day were taking a month or longer.

Again, we conducted a survey, which created a further piece of insight: the countries closer to the corporate center were unhappier—significantly so—than those further away. So we started gathering data to find out what was going on.

We found that the countries that were further away had greater delegated accountabilities than those closer to home and that these accountabilities were clearer. Indeed, countries located near the corporate center often had roles that sat partly in the center and partly in the country. This had not mattered when decision making was quick, but as the company grew, it mattered a lot. So the solution here was to clarify where each role sat and what decision-making authority it held (in fact, more oversight was needed, rather than less, for some of the far-flung operations).

Effectively, as we explained to the CEO, the company was trying to operate a large corporation using the governance structure of a small start-up. For example, any decision on point-of-sale signage in any retailer was being decided by the CEO himself for countries near the head office. This clearly was not sustainable beyond a certain organizational size! The company now needed to prepare itself to grow at scale. We learned the importance of looking at each geographical location (and, indeed, each function and business area), as the situation is never uniform, and then triangulating the findings with facts before deciding on how to fix the issues.

. . .

A Better Way

Returning to John and Amelia's reorganization of their multinational utility: how might this step have played out differently? Let's look at an alternative scenario.

Amelia has the clarity she needs on the reorganization's objectives. The next step is to understand the patient that she will be operating on: which parts are healthy and which parts diseased. She gathers her wider team together to list the organization's anatomy. She makes sure to cover people, process, and structure issues and to consider every department of the company. For example, for capital projects, she lists the following:

- Capabilities of internal capital project teams (people)

- Capabilities of engineering, construction, and procurement contractors (people)

- Investment decisions in the corporate center (process)

- Capital project planning (process)

- Capital project execution (process)

- Organizational structure for capital projects (with accountability in the business units) (structure)

- Clarity of roles for different staff involved in capital projects (structure)

She does this for all other areas of the business: retail, trading, operations and maintenance, procurement, and back office. Pretty soon, she has a list of forty potential strengths and weaknesses. Although she knows a lot about her company, the participation of her extended team of experts from each part of the business proves essential, both to highlight a number of areas she had not thought of and to make sure that each item is expressed in a way that ordinary staff will understand.

Next, Amelia sits down to think about the best way to deliver her diagnostic. For the leaders of the company, she arranges interviews and prints out the issues on playing cards, so that each interviewee can sort them into one of three piles on a game board: "Real strength" (limited to five cards), "Not an issue," and "Weakness" (again limited to five cards). This process takes twenty minutes, with the remainder of the one-hour interview focused on understanding the interviewee's choices of strengths and weaknesses. At the end of the interview, Amelia asks each leader for five recommendations of frontline staff who could also be interviewed on the issues by her team.

For the wider workforce, Amelia devises a quiz using an internet survey tool that enables the participants to sort the cards electronically. She also provides space for respondents to add comments. The respondents' geographic locations, business units, and level are recorded to aid analysis, but otherwise the survey is anonymous, to encourage candor. She sends the survey to a random selection of two hundred staff members who together represent all the major dimensions of the business. The survey goes out on a Monday, with a deadline set at the end of the week. (Amelia figures that with the pressure of operations, the surveys will either be done immediately or not at all, so giving a longer time frame does not help.) She monitors the number of respondents throughout the week, and with some follow-up from herself and the leaders whose divisions have completed few surveys, she gets a 60 percent response rate. She decides to extend the survey for a further two days the following week and, with some more chasing, reaches an almost 80 percent response rate.

At the same time, Amelia asks her extended team to conduct further analysis on the performance gaps identified in step 1. She starts by holding a workshop with them to explain the concept of *value-driver trees* (a breakdown of each unit's profitability by its components), which highlight the people costs and the capabilities for growing revenues. Given the practical culture in the company, she does this through two worked examples from one part of the business that she prepares before: one for the US business as a whole and one for the central finance function. The team is then asked to analyze the financial results of each business unit and function to understand what is driving costs and revenues and where performance in one unit lags another. She gives her team two weeks to complete the analysis.

After three weeks, Amelia is ready to share the results not only with John, the CEO, but also with his entire leadership team. Instead of the usual boring company presentation, Amelia tries a different approach. For the hour before the regular management meeting, she invites the leadership team to the boardroom, where she has hung posters summarizing the results. She has structured the material, splitting it into the top five insights across the company:

1. The United States and Europe have different challenges.

2. The leadership is much more optimistic than the workforce.

3. Processes are a bigger issue than structure.

4. Potential revenue opportunities are as big as cost savings.

5. The corporate center has a different view of the strengths and weaknesses than do the business units.

On the posters, she provides charts summarizing the survey and quotes that bring the messages to life (she takes care to include only points that have been mentioned a number of times in the quotes). She asks the CEO and other leaders to walk around the room, read the posters in whichever order they like, and ultimately come to their own conclusions on what the material means.

The leaders are struck by the messages in the posters—some of which they had not realized before. John sums up his reflections at the end of the session, and the leadership agrees. Afterward, Amelia suggests sharing the detailed findings with the wider workforce. This suggestion is a step too far for John, however: he worries that the information may reduce confidence in the company and even leak into the press. He does, however, agree to put out a summary communication on the findings to show employees that their input was worthwhile.

How to Handle Communications in Step 2

Remember that, as in step 1, communications in step 2 must start from the needs of your audience.

- **Staff and leadership needs:** This is the step when your reorg team starts to interact with the organization, asking for analyses and interviewing people. The staff will wonder why this is happening. And if they seem to be involved in the process but their peers are not, the participants may worry that their jobs in particular are threatened. If either leaders or staff start to believe that their roles are threatened, the most skilled and highest-potential people (those who can easily get jobs with your competitors) will start to dust off their CVs and investigate other options. If leaders find themselves shut out of the process, they may also start surreptitiously undermining the reorg. In addition, because employees often—indeed, should—have friendly relationships with suppliers, customers, and other outside stakeholders, you may find news leaking into the outside word.

- **What to communicate:** From the previous step, you will know which areas of the organization most need investigation and which do not. If you have followed our advice in this chapter, you will also be looking for strengths in the organization as well as weaknesses, and this will influence the reaction in the organization (much of the communication difficulties in this step stem from the team's only investigating "problems"). At the beginning of this step, you should announce that your reorganization team will be contacting people in the organization for help and which areas of the organization will be the focus. You also need to explain why these areas are the focus: if you don't fill that vacuum, people are likely to assume that you are starting there because they are the worst or will be cut the deepest. You need to equip your management, reorg, and sales teams with agreed-on Q and As with which they can answer internal and external queries. At the end of the step, you should share the results of your diagnosis—at the very least, the headlines. This shows that the people's participation was not wasted and reinforces your commitment to protect the strengths of the company if changes are needed.

- **How to communicate:** In addition to an overall communication to the organization from the CEO or leader of the unit in question, you should also have all the leaders brief their own teams if they are likely to be contacted.

As highlighted at the beginning of the book, it is critical to track whether communications are being read, what the responses are, what questions are raised, and what answers are given. Your reorg project manager needs to get into the regular habit of asking at project meetings, "How many people received the last communication?" and "What was the reaction?" If the manager does not enforce this practice of checking for reception and feedback, it's quite likely that he or she will focus entirely on transmitting messages and forget to provide intelligence on what the results were.

Step 2 Summary

Pitfalls

- Focusing only on weaknesses

- Listening only to leaders

- Relying on hearsay

Winning Ways

- Identify strengths to preserve

- Make sure you hear everyone's view

- Triangulate with analysis

How to Use These Ideas in Your Organization

- Start by defining the elements of the current organization that you want to test, with input from experts across the organization. Define a structured way to test what the strengths and weaknesses are—for example, through a card sort, a survey, or social media. Make sure that your approach leads to input from across the organization: from the most senior leaders to the front line, across different geographic locations, and between the corporate center and different business units.

- Make sure that you understand the drivers of performance gaps—in particular, the activities that drive people costs. Remember that to reduce people costs sustainably, you need to change or reduce activities. Take care to consider the implications of reduced people costs (in office space, facilities, training, travel, etc.) so that you can address these, too. Triangulate between different sources of data to ensure that you have a robust fact base. We've included in appendix D a template for identifying what really matters in your organization; it is similar to figure 4-1.

- Determine the most powerful way of sharing the findings of your diagnostic with the leadership of the company (e.g., through a gallery walk rather than a straightforward presentation). Use the raw data, but organize it into themes to make it easier to understand. Consider which parts of the material can be shared more widely throughout the organization. At least share a summary of the findings so that people can see that their feedback has been listened to.

5

Step 3

Choose from Multiple Options

"Yes, that is THE solution . . ."

Now we come to what many people see as the most important and complex part of a reorganization: choosing the new organizational model. Without underestimating its importance, you should have realized by now that the first two steps are just as important as this one: many reorganizations fail by going to step 3 too fast. You will also see how life only gets more complicated hereafter! Since the most critical element of step 3 is making a choice, it is imperative that you understand the best way to get decisions made in your organization. As Hannah Meadley-Roberts, the director of the president's office at the European Bank of Reconstruction and Development, told us: "When we changed our structure, we had to be thoughtful about our culture. When we started, we tried to do too much by consensus building but then realized that, here, you have to get some decisions on the structure made top-down and then, when the dust has settled, engage leaders in defining how to apply those decisions in different areas of the bank."

But before you launch directly into step 3, please answer the following questions to see how you are doing with your current reorg or how you fared in the past.

Which areas of the organization did you consider?

0: A high-level concept (e.g., a high-level org chart), not fully broken down into exact reporting lines.

1: Organizational structure (lines and boxes).

2: Organizational structure and people (their numbers, capabilities, and behaviors).

3: Organizational people, process, and structure.

To what degree did you consider a number of genuine options (all of which could work)?

0: From the beginning, we knew we needed to move to one target model (e.g., go functional, or reorganize around markets).

1: We considered three options with pros and cons; one of the options was clearly the best.

2: We considered several options, all of which could have worked for us.

3: We considered detailed options for different parts of the organization (not just overarching concepts).

How did you deal with leadership discomfort and debate?

0: We limited the debate to a smaller group of similarly thinking leaders and helpers until we were ready to talk to other leaders.

1: We interviewed all leaders and tried to incorporate their views into the chosen solution.

2: We included all leaders in a debate on the preferred option, after we had first done the preparatory work.

3: We had multiple leadership debates along the way, so we built the solution as we went along, not all at the end.

A Better Way

By now, you know the drill (unless you have skipped straight to this step—in which case, please go back and read the previous two steps; they are important, as you will see). Add up your score and reflect on it. A score of 7 to 9 means you are well on track. A 5 or more is not bad, and below that, you need the lessons of this chapter.

Now, let's see how you compare with Amelia.

Amelia is having a bad day. Now, every time she hears the word *reorg*, she feels a shiver creep up her spine. Despite the progress in understanding her company's strengths and weaknesses, she is starting to feel that the design of the new organization is becoming disconnected from her original objectives.

Earlier in the day, Amelia and John held a meeting in the boardroom with two external consultants, Kevin and Al, who had been recommended by the CEO. Their company works with many utilities and other energy clients, so Amelia hoped that they would be able to help her in designing the new organization. Amelia and the consultants spent over two hours going through a set of case studies of other utilities' reporting line structures. The problem was that Amelia could not understand how the companies worked in practice: all the structures looked pretty much the same to her. Kevin and Al also seemed unclear on the detail—they could easily describe the major differences between the models at a high level, but were unable to provide much information on how accountabilities were divided up and how many people worked in each part of the organization: two critical things that Amelia needs to know.

Nonetheless, John felt that they had had a constructive session, sketching out alternative reporting line structures on the whiteboard. On Kevin and Al's advice, they focused on the top three layers of the organization. They looked at a few alternatives and then settled on a model the consultants called a *functional-matrix* model. During this discussion, Amelia realized that, in this model, additional senior leaders would be required (a new global head of capital projects and a new head of safety). She worried about how this need would fit with the reorganization's primary objective to reduce cost: how would people feel if the first act of the reorg would be to add to the senior head count? However, Kevin and Al assured her that the efficiencies of the new model would justify the investment: the companies from the case examples that used this kind of organization scored higher than theirs in industry cost benchmarking. John seemed reassured.

After the meeting with the consultants, John convenes a telephone conference with his closest allies in the organization—young men and women who, like him, are impatient for change. Amelia, as the project manager, is, of course, also invited. However, John makes sure to exclude the old guard: the current country managers who are set in their ways. He explains to the group that he wants to keep the reorganization secret, work with his trusted confederates and the consultants, and then "socialize" the answer—as the consultants had put it—with his other reports later.

Despite the restricted nature of the telephone conference, only a few hours later, Amelia receives a call from one of the country market-unit managing directors, Gavin, asking her about the new functional model. Someone at the teleconference must have already leaked the information or otherwise spoken loosely! It is not surprising that Gavin was one of the first to know: given his long service, he is extremely well connected in the organization. Amelia assures Gavin that there are no plans for him to move from his current role and that the main results of the reorg—beyond the need to reduce costs—will be the creation of some new central functions to provide best-practice advice. Amelia tells Gavin that these changes will only be helpful to him and his team. In any case, she adds, the details are still to be worked out, and the CEO will convene a full meeting of the management team once the plans are more solid.

Amelia sits at her desk, reviewing the work with the consultants and her notes from the call with Gavin. She starts to worry. How will this new organizational structure deliver the cost-reduction targets required? How will the other leaders and staff react to the new functional roles? How will the new head of safety solve the issue of blurred accountabilities, given that these accountabilities are much deeper down in the organization? And how would the new head of the central projects—a position they had not previously considered—influence the work of teams on the ground if these teams still reported to the country managing directors, regardless of the dotted lines that the consultants had drawn on the new org chart?[1] Amelia is confused. She has heard that reorganizations are not happy experiences. Now she is starting to see why.

Does Amelia's experience seem painfully familiar to you? And has she done anything particularly foolish? Not really; she has followed the recipe used for the vast majority of reorganizations. But Amelia does not realize that her day is much worse than she thought. She and her advisers have made three cardinal mistakes, setting the stage for even bigger problems for the future.

Pitfall 1: Skipping the First Two Steps

Skipping steps is one pitfall that Amelia and her team have avoided. But it is one that many, many other reorg leaders fall into: they fail to define the value of the reorganization or to link it to the company's particular challenges. Instead, they start by designing a new model based on the latest theory or best practices drawn from competitors and analogous industries. In doing so, they create a cookie-cutter organization with no clear benefits. At best, the change will deliver no value but will also do limited harm. At worst, it will face organ rejection. The remedy is clear: you must complete the first two steps properly. The previous two chapters explain why these steps are important (hopefully, you haven't jumped straight to reading this one!).

Pitfall 2: Focusing Only on Lines and Boxes

So far, Amelia, the CEO, and their advisers have only discussed one aspect of reorganization: how the roles in the structure will report to each other. As Lawrence Gosden of Thames Water told us: "Thinking about boxes and lines is easy and tangible and appeals to people who like to get things done quickly. But you have to get beyond that to understanding business processes and then, beyond that, to discussing people and culture."

To understand why it is important to go beyond drawing lines and boxes on an org chart, consider the example of a soccer team. Your team—let's call it Leeds United—is performing badly. As the latest manager (the team has been through quite a few), you need to drive improvements. Let's say that you follow the typical approach of business reorgs and simply change the organizational structure, say, from a 4-4-2 formation on the field to a 4-3-3 formation. You base the new formation on the fact that Barcelona, one of the best teams in the world, plays with the latter arrangement (a best practice).

Would this changed lineup solve your problems? Of course not. You also need to address two other areas of the organization. First, you need to improve the skills and behaviors of the players—by training those you have and perhaps signing some new players. You can also think of ways to motivate the players better (e.g., in 1961, the then Leeds United manager, Don Revie, changed the colors of the shirts from the civic blue and yellow to the white of Real Madrid to encourage his players to play more like the Spanish club). Second, you need to improve the way that your footballers play together: how they pass, build up attacks, get back to defend, and so forth (in business, we typically call this *processes*). These two nonstructural factors are probably more important than the team's organizational structure, given that you can find both good and bad teams that play in a 4-3-3 formation, just as much as in a 4-4-2 (whatever your opinion of the best practice may be). In fact, the right formation is very much determined by the players and the way they play, not the other way around.

Just like soccer teams, all organizations have three dimensions to consider: people, processes, and structure. Other organization practitioners use different frameworks (and a number have even written whole books about them), but they pretty much cover the same ground. The important thing is to have a comprehensive set of organizational components to cover (table 5-1).

We contend that, of the three areas, people and processes are the most important and the most neglected. The reason for this is simple. The rationale for reorganizations, expressed in plain English, is to encourage a large number of people to work in a different way to deliver more value (higher revenues, lower cost, a better return on investment, etc.). Forget about all the jargon that you hear (target operating models, best practices, organizational

TABLE 5-1

Areas to address in a reorganization when choosing between several options

Dimension	Areas to address in a reorganization
People	• Number of people
	• Capabilities and experience
	• Mind-sets and behaviors (including motivation)
Processes	• Management processes (strategy, risk, capital allocation, business planning, performance management, people attraction and development, etc.)
	• Business processes (technology and R&D, capital projects, operations and maintenance, marketing, sales, etc.)
	• IT systems
Structure	• Governance and delegation of authority
	• Reporting lines
	• Role descriptions or job profiles

development, change management, and the like), and keep this simple objective in mind.

This is not to say that structure doesn't matter: if accountabilities are divided unclearly between different roles and teams, it may be only a change to the structure can clarify them (as you will see in one of the examples to follow). However, by simply changing someone's boss (or, in a large organization, the boss's boss's boss), you will do little to change the way that person works day to day. If you come into work tomorrow and your boss changes from Judy to Ahmad, will that really change how you spend your day? Probably not. This simple point is usually overlooked. As the reorganization fizzles out a few management layers below them, leaders will often console themselves by saying, "This reorganization manages risk effectively because it does not impact the front line." They may as well say, "This reorganization will deliver no value because the front line will see no need to change and will continue to work tomorrow in just the same way as it does today."

Pitfall 3: Imposing One Solution

Egged on by the consultants, Amelia and the CEO have also fallen into the common trap of selecting a single solution according to what "best-practice" competitors do. Would any business leader follow a similar approach for any other area of business life? Imagine copy-pasting a competitor's strategy for entering China, using a few pages of PowerPoint as justification!

There are likely to be many options that would work for Amelia's utility company (as well as many bad options that would not work and that she should avoid). Considering a range of possibilities would help her and John see the different benefits and risks of each option, to weigh them consciously against each other, and to choose the option that best fits the company's situation. Indeed, considering multiple options often results in a final recommendation that brings together the best of several options. When a single option is chosen at the start, our experience is that bad things happen. At some stage, too late in the process, leaders point to the foregone benefits from alternative approaches. The project team may then be asked to tweak the design to deliver some of these foregone benefits. This typically leads to last-minute adjustments that have not been well thought through and a design that is a bit of a jumble—with things that no one really understands stuck on at the last moment.

The process by which you take the inputs from steps 1 and 2 and create a design that addresses them is one of the toughest challenges in a reorganization. It is the first point that requires not just deductive thinking ($X + Y = Z$) but also inductive thinking ("How about we try something very different, such as A?"). This is where experience is helpful, but we believe that you can still learn the *science* of doing this for your first or second reorganization. Essentially, there are two different approaches:

- **Top down:** Develop a number of concepts, making sure that they outline how the model would work (people and process) as well as what it looks like (structure). At the same time, define about five criteria against which you can assess those options according to steps 1 and 2 (e.g., the extent to which it reduces costs, tightens accountabilities, minimizes the human cost, and fits the existing culture of the organization) to compare the different concepts. This top-down approach works best if the company needs to navigate a fundamental shift or if the current organization is fundamentally broken, or both. Table 5-2 shows some typical top-down options for companywide reorgs, when you might use them, and the challenges of each option to manage. There is no one silver bullet. You have to pick an option that best suits your strategy and company culture.

- **Bottom up:** Instead of developing overarching concepts, brainstorm a number of improvement ideas to deliver the required benefits and address organizational weaknesses. These can relate to people, process, or structure, or some combination of those (merge teams A and B, remove a layer of management, cut the frequency of activity X by 50 percent, improve process Y, etc.). Rate these ideas in terms of their benefits, costs (including human costs), and feasibility. Through management discussions, decide which of these

TABLE 5-2

Potential top-down options

Type of organization	Description	Use if you want . . .	Be careful to manage the challenges of . . .
Geographic/ market based	• Series of local businesses, each with a local head, and with all necessary functions	• P&L ownerships/ focus on margins • Responsiveness to local conditions	• Reluctance to accept global approaches/ tendency to reinvent wheel
Value-chain based	• Separate units for each step of business (e.g., R&D, product development, sales), covering all geographies	• Focus on long- and short-term performance, P&L ownership (even if some P&Ls negative)	• Managing across interfaces and prioritizing across time frames
Functional based	• Separate units for each activity (e.g., capital projects, operations, business development, finance, etc.), covering all geographies	• Synergies within functions • Improved quality/ safety	• Lack of P&L ownership • Delays in decision making
Product based	• Separate teams for each product, all with necessary functions	• Speed of product development • Interdisciplinary collaboration	• Interface issues where multiple products serve same customer • Local customization (especially with sales)
Project/issue based	• Teams organized around projects/ issues (e.g., in an IT consulting or construction organization, or a government department)	• Activities aligned to client needs/ revenues • Walls between teams	• Lack of learning over time • Falling in love with a project (not killing bad ideas)

ideas to take ahead and which to leave aside. Where an improvement idea is selected, the organization changes. Where it is not, the organization stays the same. This approach works if the current organization works well in the main but needs adjustment in certain areas. Table 5-3 shows some potential bottom-up ideas covering both effectiveness and efficiency. Although, in the case of bottom up, the secret is not to develop generic options, but very concrete options that fit the situation at hand. That is the main benefit of this approach.

In both of these approaches, if you need radical change, there are benefits in seeking external expertise and innovative ideas. You might turn to colleagues in other organizations, academics, the literature, or consultants who may have seen different approaches that could inspire your future design. No matter who or what you consult, any design needs to be tailored to your organization: we strongly advise against the copy-paste approach.

TABLE 5-3

Potential bottom-up options

Effectiveness	Efficiency
• Replace/rotate leaders	• Increase spans of management control/remove management layers
• Appoint senior leader/committee to drive topic	• Insource/outsource activities
• Train staff	• Introduce lean processes
• Set targets and metrics	• Remove activities
• Redesign processes	• Reduce frequency of activities
• Clarify accountabilities	• Centralize/offshore activities
• Clarify interface between one team and another	• Automate activities
• Consolidate responsibility from many teams to one	

We offer examples of both approaches below. In Amelia's case, she is taking a top-down approach (as most substantive reorganizations do). But in light of the results of steps 1 and 2, a bottom-up approach would be worth considering, because only parts of her organization work badly.

Pitfall 4: Going Around Difficult Leaders

It can be very tempting to try to sidestep difficult leaders. As one of the executives involved in a reorg told us, "We needed more support along the way from our senior stakeholders and to bring them along the journey, but instead, we did it in isolation from them, as that was what we were primed to do." But avoiding difficult stakeholders is always a mistake. John tried to do it, and what happened? One of those difficult leaders found out, and Amelia and her team were already on the defensive. This always happens: you think you can keep your plans secret, but the office rumor mill is too strong for you.

As the saying goes, it is better to have leaders in the tent than outside. It makes the discussions more difficult, but including everyone has two clear benefits. First, leaders see that their opinions are listened to and respected, which is more important than the final result (which may or may not be their preferred option). At the end of one particularly controversial reorganization, we were told by one business leader, "I did not agree with the design we decided on, but I cannot fault the process that got us to this decision, and I do feel that all my concerns were heard." This was one of the highest pieces of praise we have received.

The second benefit of including difficult leaders is that you may learn some things that none of your fellow travelers would have pointed out. In doing so, you may develop a greater appreciation of the value of these leaders. As Nancy McKinstry, the CEO of Wolters Kluwer, told us: "I was quite surprised by which leaders succeeded in the reorganization. They were not always the ones that I thought would succeed at the beginning." Of course, some of your team may be so allergic to change that you and they need to part company—but the time to do this is at the next step. Alienating them now will add no benefits.

Rob Rosenberg, HR director of DHL Supply Chain, told us, "Regardless of org structures, unless leaders begin to trust one another and take risks and chances openly with each other, it does not matter what blueprints you put in organizationally; they won't work. I recall having to be quite patient in working through blueprints and rounds and rounds of discussions with leaders, but this is now proving to be very useful, as they bought into the decisions we made and felt part of them."

In our experience, some of the leaders who are most antagonistic to an organizational change at the start of a process can become the people most committed to it later on when their input has been considered or their positions are changed. By definition those leaders are engaged in the process (far worse are leaders who are passive through the process) and, if properly listened to, can become hugely supportive of the change.

. . .

We will now share a few cases that illustrate winning ways to solve the pitfalls highlighted above. For the first pitfall—that is, skipping steps 1 and 2—there is a simple answer: don't do it!

Winning Way 2: Cover People, Process, and Structure

The principles of this book cover both large and small businesses. To illustrate this, take the case of a family-owned general dentistry company. The head of this business, Maryam, bought a predominantly private, two-surgery dental practice in her hometown. The practice that she purchased had a firm base of satisfied patients, but it was losing money. There were two other dental surgery practices nearby, limiting the degree to which she could attract new patients and therefore grow revenues.

After investigating the accounts and meeting with the staff, Maryam concluded that the efficiency of the business needed to improve. However, she was adamant that, at the same time, the quality of the patient care should not be affected and, in fact, could be improved. Maryam set a target for profitability using benchmarks of similar practices, kindly provided by her accountant (see step 1). She then diagnosed three main issues behind the underperformance: poor utilization of staff (there were large gaps in the dentists' days), overspending on unnecessary stock, and a lack of communication with patients outside their appointments, leading to lengthy periods between patient visits (see step 2). Addressing the patient-communication issue would not only improve revenues but also improve patient health.

Fortunately, one of Maryam's friends, Andy, had experience in successfully turning around the performance of his own dental business. At lunch one day, Andy explained to Maryam how he achieved this. First of all, he established the position of an office manager (someone he trusted: his wife) and had all the receptionists and nurses report to her. He also introduced a hygienist, who was able to pick up on the practice's growing workload, delivering simple procedures more economically than the dentists could. The dentists were then freed up to focus on procedures that were more complex. These measures, Andy assured Maryam, are now regarded as best practice. Andy had recently attended a national conference in which he learned that all the best dental businesses are implementing these improvements.

Should Maryam implement Andy's best-practice organizational model? Certainly, it worked for him. But Maryam had her doubts. Although the primary aim of any dental practice is the care and treatment of the patients, it is still a business and needs to survive. Andy's practice was three times the size of her own, focused mainly on a public-sector contract, and was facing growing pains rather than efficiency problems. Were Maryam to implement Andy's advice, there would be no improvement to how her staff worked. Such a reorg would only create unnecessary hierarchy and envy and raise the cost base.

Instead, Maryam decided to develop her own ideas according to the particular issues she had identified. She developed an improved process for booking patients, working with the receptionist to help him understand what is required (a process and people solution). This improved utilization, but not sufficiently to close all the gaps in the dentists' diaries. She therefore reduced the hours of the dentists and nurses (closing one of the surgeries for two days a week) to make better use of resources (a people solution). Maryam next turned her attention to costs. She changed the process for ordering stock, requiring her personal sign-off for orders above certain volume and price (process). And she trained the receptionist and nurses to locate and utilize stock already in the practice before reaching for the order book (people). Finally, with regard to communications with patients, she updated the receptionist's role description and set clear expectations for calling patients (this last step, alone, is a structure solution).

With these changes, Maryam managed to triple the profits of the business in just one year and improve the quality of treatment and care for her patients (through better communications and an increase in regular checkups). She also improved the capabilities of her staff through training. Maryam is now buying another, similar practice to expand her business.

Winning Way 3: Explore Different Options

Our work with a European water company shows the benefits of coming up with more than one solution to the challenges leaders face in step 2. François, a seasoned water industry professional, had just been appointed head of field operations. As he surveyed his new organization, he realized that it was made up of a disparate patchwork of legacy organizations, each with its own structure, ways of working, and culture: a wastewater networks team, where many activities were outsourced to contractors; a clean-water networks team, which also used contractors, but carried out many more activities in-house; and a maintenance team, responsible for maintaining the water treatment works, sewage treatment works, and pumping stations. As an added complication, the clean-water networks team in particular was heavily unionized. Steps 1 and 2 had identified a 10 percent cost-reduction challenge, together with the need to improve management capabilities to run operations. François was used to driving efficiencies: he and his team already had ideas on the changes required. However, he wanted to make sure that his group considered a full set of options, that the complex process of developing an organizational concept was well managed, and that there was an appropriate forum for ideas to be discussed.

A team was therefore put together with managers from each of the different business areas, supported by us and a few other consultants. By holding discussions and brainstorming sessions with leaders and experts from the different business areas, the team generated a long list of potential bottom-up organizational changes. We even met with a union official to hear his ideas for addressing management and contractor inefficiencies. Each idea was explored in detail to uncover how it would work and what benefits and risks it would bring. Each week, the team would bring the potential organizational changes to a decision-making committee, which would decide which of these suggestions to take forward, which to discard, and which required further analysis and investigation before a decision could be made. The committee comprised not only the head of field operations but also the leaders of other organizations (water production, waste process, and capital projects), as changes to field operations would also have an impact on these three other organizations.

The ideas selected by this process included merging the management of the clean-water and wastewater network teams in four regions (versus the original six for the previous separate organizations). The frontline staff, of course, had to remain separated (you cannot start interfering with clean-water pipes after working with sewage!). However, there were significant management savings. To make this idea work, the process for planning, scheduling, and delivering work also had to be standardized across clean water and wastewater, and managers who came from one business had to be trained in the peculiarities of the other. In the maintenance team, too, the management of clean-water and wastewater activities, previously separated, were also merged, leading to significant savings. Again, process and people changes accompanied the structural changes.

Other ideas included removing a whole layer of middle management in the network teams (with savings partly reinvested in a training course to improve the quality of frontline managers); the amalgamation of two teams that were both focused on regulatory water testing; reducing the management numbers in the maintenance team to reflect better spans of control; merging the work of technicians in the maintenance team and those working in sewage treatment works; and improving the efficiency of clean-water network technicians through process improvements. These two final ideas were piloted in one region to confirm that the savings identified on paper could be delivered in practice. Given the high degree of unionization in the clean-water networks team, and the management's concern about reducing the people cost of the change, savings in this area were achieved by insourcing other work previously carried out by the contractors. This also required a rewiring of the process and the retraining of staff.

One important point was the close involvement of HR in this process. Because the company was based in the European Union, we had to follow EU employment legislation (the regulations, incidentally, do not prevent you from making such changes; they just reemphasize the need to follow a proper process) (see appendix C). And because the need for savings was urgent, we worked quickly, delivering end products in the form needed by HR for consultations (whether this was an updated role profile in Word or an organizational structure drawn in a particular way in PowerPoint). In this way, we avoided creating masses of PowerPoint presentations that HR would later have to translate into the required formats later.

As with the majority of reorganizations—especially those that include significant savings, the loss of people's jobs, and shifting power of leaders—progress was not always smooth and many of the conversations were painful and required substantial time and care from leaders. Displaced employees were offered substantial support in finding new roles outside the company. Occasionally, operational emergencies prevented leaders from attending a meeting. Sometimes, follow-up meetings were required outside the decision meetings when agreement could not be reached. All this notwithstanding, the weekly decision meetings provided a focus for the debate and decision making; managers fully led the work, and the handling of improvement ideas one at a time— rather than wrapped up into one overarching concept—kept the discussion focused.

Winning Way 4: Have the Leadership Debate Now

The importance of the leadership debate was made very clear to us by work we did together for a global media company. This company was navigating a seismic shift in the industry: from publishing—a high-margin but declining industry—to software, a lower-margin but fast-growing business. The experience not only showed the importance of leadership engagement but also illustrated how to identify issues quickly across processes, people, and structure (step 2) and the importance of developing different options, this time from the top down.

The company had grown through acquiring many smaller, local businesses. As with many media companies, the prevailing belief was that this was a purely talent-driven business and that processes and structure were much less important (one exception to the rule that structure is the predominant focus). This belief had prevented the company from consolidating activities and standardizing processes. Language was also a very important consideration, up to a point. Content had to be created, or at least translated, into local languages. And the editorial and sales staff had to be fluent in the local language. In a number of countries, below middle management, English was not commonly spoken. But the top two layers of management in every country were fluent in English, which was the company language, and many of the systems could be standardized even when language and content could not.

The company was defined by strong local leadership, and each business unit (whether in the United States, Europe, China, or India) was responsible for selling the full range of products. The challenge with this arrangement was that the company was not as focused on specific customer segments as it could have been and was unable to capture the benefits of global scale in these segments (each local unit reinvented the wheel for its customer segments).

The CEO realized that a change in the organization was required and asked us to help. Her team had already developed a potential future structure, in which central teams were created to develop new products and encourage the shift to software in each of the four areas of business but which otherwise left the local businesses pretty much as they were. Our role was to work out if this design was right—though we only had four weeks to do so. Fortunately, we had the benefit of a strong full-time client team, with a representative from the business and from HR.

Before doing anything else, we familiarized ourselves with the value opportunity, reading recent work from the company's strategy team (step 1). Next, we conducted a rapid diagnostic of the company's current strengths and weaknesses (step 2). We did this through a card-sort exercise (see chapter 4) in interviews with twenty corporate and local leaders from across the company and a wider survey of staff. The diagnostic, in itself, was also a way to engage with leaders about the change.

Through the diagnostic, we learned that the company's local connections were a strength that needed to be preserved—especially in Europe, where there were not only language but also content differences across countries. Capable country-level leaders were another strength. At the same time, we learned that most of the existing processes were ignored and that this attitude seemed to be accepted in the culture—meaning that a purely process solution to the problem would not work. Finally, the leaders told us that while they understood the need for change, they were confused about what the proposed central teams would really do. Some managers saw the proposal as an incremental change; others as a fundamental shift.

Early on in the process, we agreed with the CEO that, rather than just improving the existing straw-man answer, we would also create alternatives for her and her team to choose from. The forum for this choice would be a workshop—a global meeting of twelve of the company's top business leaders. We defined four organizational models: full business-line division, revenue-focused division, global product developer, and center of competence. These options broadly ranged from more radical centralization (full business-line division) to less.

As it turned out, the fourth, and least centralized, option, which limited the role of the divisions to developing global platforms and products and sourcing global content, was discounted by the CEO, as she did not believe that it would drive the change required. This incremental option had been the one most favored by the company's leadership (naturally, because few people like change, so they often lean toward the option that affects them the least). Ruling it out therefore changed the game considerably. Remember, it is important to involve leadership teams in the choice, but the leader needs to set the boundaries of acceptable options; the process is not a democracy!

Our challenge then was to bring the three remaining options to life for leaders who had been confused by the debate so far and who, like most business leaders, were more comfortable with day-to-day business than ethereal organizational concepts. This also meant illustrating the options in terms of people and processes, not just structure.

On the question of people, we defined five critical roles that would generally be found in each of the three options, but which would act very differently in each: a head of one of the four business lines, a global marketing director, a regional managing director, a country CEO, and a sales and marketing manager. For each role, we created three "days in the life"—one for each option—showing how the role would differ for a full business-line division, a revenue-focused division, and a global product developer. We also developed indicative role profiles and pie charts to show how much time the person fulfilling the role would spend in each option. For example, the role of the country CEO would no longer exist in the full business-line division option. For the revenue-focused division, the country CEO would be responsible for local tailoring of products, sourcing of local content, distribution, and managing customer relationships, but would have no responsibility for strategy, sales, or platform or product development. And in the global-products option, the country CEO would spend his or her time on local sales and marketing, distribution, and customer relationships. In all three cases, the role would be very different from the role in the previous organization, where the country CEO controlled all activities.

For processes, with the help of experts from across the business, we drew a chart of the overarching business process that would apply equally across all locations and business lines: from strategy to local business plans, development of platforms and products, local tailoring of products, sourcing of global and local content, marketing, sales, distribution, customer relationships, and back-office support. For each of the three options, we defined the responsibilities of different organizations along our overarching process: with the business-line division, country business, and support services all represented by a different color. This chart provided a simple, visual explanation of how responsibilities would differ in each of the three options and where the handovers between different parts of the organization would take place. Often it is in these handovers where organizations experience problems, whether they stem from conflict between different parts of the organization or topics falling between the gaps.

Finally, we showed how each of the options would play out as an organizational structure (reporting lines). At this stage, we used schematic rather than detailed organizational charts, as the idea was to outline the concept, not to debate about the reporting lines and roles of particular leaders. This enabled us to identify the pain points associated with each of the options. For example, in the case of the full business-line division, the local businesses would not exist anymore (they would be divided up between the global divisions), but a whole series of local responsibilities would remain: representing the local legal entity (the country CEO), managing local support services that were not reporting to global shared services, managing the office and other property, and providing the social focus for the working community. This is actually a very common challenge in any company shifting from a local, country, or asset organization to a global one based on business lines, value chain, or function. In this case, we suggested that these functions should be owned in country by the business line that represented the biggest (or fastest growing) game in town. One issue that we had to clarify (and that many companies get confused by) was the difference between centralizing the reporting and centralizing the location of activities. For example, sales staff could report to a central function, but they would always have to be located locally, speaking the local language. On the other hand, the creation of an IT platform could be centralized under one manager and in one physical location, as long as there was a clear way to take into account local needs.

A document containing these options and the associated descriptions was sent to the twelve participants for the leadership workshop for them to read ahead of time. In planning this workshop, we were faced with another major challenge: how to ensure that the company's leaders, most of whom had only experienced one way of working—in a geographically focused business—would be able to open up their eyes to the other options available. Our chosen solution was a technique called *appreciative inquiry*, an organizational approach developed by David Cooperrider and Suresh Srivastva in the late 1980s. In a nutshell, appreciative inquiry focuses on the positives of different options and is based on the observation that when people focus on positives, they tend to have a much more open mind and to be more creative. Finding problems is generally an easier activity and can come later.

In particular, our objective was to avoid the typical situation in a reorganization (and one with which you may be familiar), where the CEO and corporate leaders argue their thesis of greater change, the local businesses argue their antithesis of minimal change, and the consultant—like a magician pulling a rabbit from a hat—suggests the "middle option" as the appropriate synthesis. Relieved, everyone then aligns on the middle option as the least bad option that everyone can agree on. In our view, this way of reaching consensus is a mistake, as the middle option will always contain its own peculiar benefits and risks, which are rarely an arithmetic average of the other two options and can sometimes be worse than either. Moreover, an answer that almost no one wants feels like a poor basis for future progress.

On the day of the workshop, having provided a brief introduction and reminded people of the purpose of the day, we split the group into three subgroups, each covering one of the organizational options: full business-line division, revenue-focused division, and global product developer. On purpose, we placed strong-minded leaders with a particular preference in the group covering the option that they would be expected to hate. In this way, they would be forced to think themselves into an option that they had probably spent little time considering when they read the document we had prepared. Between these interested parties, we interspersed more-agnostic leaders. At this stage, we also asked the CEO to leave the room to prevent any issues of sunflower management (the bias that occurs when some staff seek to guess what their leader wants and then provide that answer, as a sunflower turns toward the sun).

We asked each group to prepare a case, advocating for the option that it had been given (with no negatives allowed). Each group would then present its case to the other groups and answer questions on it. We asked each group to tell us how its option would contribute toward three benefits: exploiting the benefits of global scale in each of the four business lines, maintaining knowledge of local markets, and promoting the shift from publishing to software. After this advocacy, the other two groups would get to shoot holes in the case, and the presenting group would have to defend it.

What we found when we ran this exercise was magical. In fact, a while later, one of the attendees jokingly accused us of employing hypnosis.

Each of the teams started to work on creating a case for its option. Since the participants, like most business leaders, were highly competitive high-achievers, the room quickly took on an adrenaline-fueled air, with flip charts produced and lists of benefits rehearsed. Released from feeling that they had to criticize the options, each team took its option and built on it: all of them created improvements to their options, making them more robust.

Going through the three presentations, which were all entertaining as well as informative, immediately made several things clear. First of all, with the most incremental option (center of competence) removed because it would have minimal impact, it was clear that all other options—including the now most incremental one (global product developer) would have a significant impact on the way the company operated. This was brought to life in particular by the process maps and day-in-the-life scenarios that we had developed (org charts on their own seldom highlight such issues). In fact, the middle option (revenue-focused division) would lead to the most conflict and complexity. At the same time, the benefits of the global product developer and revenue-focused division in meeting the criteria were not wholly convincing. Instead, it became increasingly clear through the debate, almost to the shock of the team that was presenting it, that the only option that would provide sufficient benefits to justify the disruption and the human cost of the change was the full business-line division.

For this reason, nine of the attendees, when asked after the presentations were complete, indicated a clear preference for this model. The remaining three also preferred this model, but expressed some justifiable concerns as to how the company would implement it. They were especially concerned about the disruption that it would cause colleagues, many of whose jobs would change, and the differences in mind-sets, behaviors, and capabilities required to make the option work. These concerns informed the approach to detailed design and implementation planning (to be covered later, in step 4). The CEO, who had reentered the room to hear the presentations, was shocked but also delighted, as the participants' choice was also her preferred option for very similar reasons (although the team had substantially improved it). As she told us later, "There is always more than one right answer, so the process of how you bring people along and get them behind the new organization is really important. Through the workshop, we both came to a good answer, and, more importantly perhaps, we brought our leadership team along with us."

With the input of the workshop, we were able to create draft designs for the overall business process, people, and structure of the four divisions. All in four weeks.

. . .

To reiterate the lessons from the cases above, let's return to Amelia and her bad day.

Walking out of the meeting with the two consultants, Kevin and Al, Amelia has the suspicion that the top-down concepts they have been discussing are not going to work for her company. She has learned a few good ideas from the cases, but none of them provides the full answer she needs.

Instead, Amelia decides to hold a meeting with the experts from each of the market units and functions that make up her extended team. Each of them has, of course, been developing their own ideas on how to meet the cost reduction and efficiency targets demanded by the CEO. At the beginning of the meeting, Amelia shares what she has learned about the company's competitors from the consultants. Fortunately, several people at the meeting have previously worked for competitors and are able to provide further details on how these models worked in practice (not only the high-level reporting lines, but also some of the approaches to processes and people). Amelia also reminds the attendees of the results of step 2—namely, the areas of the company that need to change and those that need to remain to maintain the company's current strengths.

Amelia uses the meeting to get a full set of bottom-up improvement ideas. She has each expert present ideas and get feedback and encouragement from the others. This generates an atmosphere of friendly competition. By the end, she has a dozen options for organizational improvements, focused on the areas where the company is either experiencing challenges or maintaining its current strengths. These ideas cover a range of people, process, and structural issues. Amelia asks the teams to detail their ideas in single-page templates that highlight the benefits of the idea (in terms of cost reduction, value improvement, and safety improvement), its risks, and what it would take to implement.

Amelia then asks the CEO, John, to call a series of weekly decision-making meetings with his management team. Of course, there is opposition, with leaders complaining that they do not have time. But Amelia is persistent, reminding them of the value of the reorganization from step 1 and the early discussion that the leadership had about the time commitment needed for this change. John backs her up, and the meetings are booked in diaries. Leaders are requested to attend in person and not to send delegates if they cannot attend. (Amelia knows that it is impossible to have this debate over the phone, and that both for confidentiality reasons and for the team to build trust, it is important to keep the membership of the group stable.)

Over the next four weeks, Amelia, John, and his leadership team work their way through the organizational options. Amelia front-loads the options that seem clear into the first meeting, and most are quickly signed off. In the next two meetings, she presents the other options: some are signed off, others are thrown out, and a third category meets a mixed reaction—Amelia and her team are asked to do further work on these. For difficult cases, she invites some of the experts to present their own ideas. Their input improves the debate, shows the leaders that their own people are contributing toward the answers, and gives the experts an opportunity for exposure to senior leaders (as most people dislike reorgs, it is a good idea to make sure that they get some benefit from their participation).

In the final meeting, Amelia recaps the decisions made to date, notably the following: opex cuts of between 5 and 30 percent in organizational units; standardized roles and processes across different market units; a new centralized trading team, with a significant upgrade to its talent (10 percent of people to be replaced); a common capital process across the business, with a central team to ensure compliance, but responsibilities still left with the country market units; and a new training program for safety, with clarified roles in the business. Amelia then shows an integrated picture of what the new organization will look like—the impact on people, the new processes, and the overall organizational structure. In particular, she highlights the amount of change that will be required to roles in the organization and the likely number of staff affected. As this is merely a summation of decisions agreed on, the CEO and his team sign off on the design, although only after a debate about the human cost of the change. This human factor is highlighted by the team as something Amelia must consider as she begins detailing the changes and planning the implementation. At the same time, in informal discussions after the meeting, Amelia notes that many leaders are starting to wonder about what the reorg means for their current position and how they will be able to implement the changes.

How to Handle Communications in Step 3

- **Staff and leadership needs:** Staff still needs to understand what the reorg means for them and when they will hear about any impact on their jobs. Step 3 will not meet these needs, because the concepts that result will not get down to this level of detail. Given this, the most important thing that staff need to hear is the timeline for action. Leaders have much more tangible needs in this step because you are now deciding the shape of the organization and the responsibilities of each of its units. No matter how much you say that you are only dealing with a design and that people assignments will come later, leaders will start thinking what this means for them (with a tendency to assume they will stay in their existing jobs—which may or may not be true). Excluding them from decision making will exacerbate this misconception, as we showed above.

- **What to communicate:** At the beginning of this step, the message you need to clearly communicate to staff is the following: what work is taking place, who will be doing it, and when the results will be announced. At the end of the step, communicate the direction implied by the concept design and when staff will know what it means for them (in step 4). Avoid the temptation to stage an exciting announcement about your new functional organization, the fantastic return on investment it will generate, or the prediction that the design will be 20 percent more efficient. You and your fellow leaders may be excited about this achievement. Your employees, by contrast, will be frightened by any discussion of efficiency savings and will be uninterested in management metrics until they know the impact on their jobs. Leaders, again, are different. At the end of this stage and the beginning of the next, you should be appointing leaders to new positions and making them responsible for delivering the detailed design, rather than resisting it. When you include leadership in this way, you may find that some leaders will not succeed with the reorg or will decide that the new organization is not for them.

- **How to communicate:** Because you are increasingly getting into the details of how each business unit or function will work and are starting to appoint leaders to reshape these units or functions, it is appropriate that, in addition to continued central communications, more and more of the communications come from the leaders of the units, tailored for their part of the organization. For the broader workforce, for whom this step is less important, a simple conference call, e-mail, or blog post with, again, a mechanism for two-way communications is sufficient at this stage. For leaders, candid one-on-one conversations are required. Again, remember to track and discuss the results of communications. What are you learning? That way, you can identify the talented manager most at risk of leaving, rather than being surprised when he or she walks out for a new job just after you have announced this person as the head of an important new business line.

Step 3 Summary

Pitfalls

- Skipping steps 1 and 2

- Focusing only on lines and boxes

- Imposing one generic solution

- Going around difficult leaders

Winning Ways

- Don't skip steps 1 and 2!

- Cover process, people, and structure

- Explore different options

- Have the leadership debate now

How to Use These Ideas in Your Organization

- Remember to focus on people and processes as much as, or more than, structure.

- Decide whether you should take a top-down or bottom-up approach to the reorganization. Remember, a top-down approach (like the global media company) is appropriate if the company is going through a seismic shift or if the organization is fundamentally broken, and a bottom-up approach (like the water company) is appropriate if the organization works well with a few select issues. If in doubt, go for the bottom-up option, as it is easier to focus on changes that add value quickly, it minimizes the human cost, and it avoids breaking anything else. Use the templates in appendix D for implementing whichever approach you decide to take.

- Use the collective wisdom in your organization. You should hold brainstorming meetings with the staff closest to the action to generate ideas for improvements. You can also draw on external consultants, especially for more-difficult reorganizations and to understand how others have approached the problem, but remember that outside ideas should only supplement the input from your own organization.

- Put a lot of thought into how to run meetings with the leadership team to understand the trade-offs and make decisions. This could be through one big meeting to decide on the top-down concept (like the media company case) or through a series of meetings to thrash through bottom-up options (as in the water company case). Whichever approach you take, think through the likely dynamics between the leaders in the room. Consider having the meeting or meetings off-site if possible to get away from day-to-day issues. Make sure that you have the active support of the project sponsor (if you are a member of the reorg team) or that you provide active support (if you are the project sponsor).

6

Step 4

Get the Plumbing and Wiring Right

"This is your road to ReOrg. Make sure to cover all the details. And stay clear of Bob, he is not changing . . ."

This is the step where you need to define how your new organization really works. It is also the step where many leaders take their foot off the gas pedal. But as you will see, step 4 is perhaps the most difficult and complex step and the one where leadership decisions are most essential for success. Even our quiz for this step is more complicated. Ironically, management consultants are typically called in for the earlier steps (which are generally easier) but almost never for this step. Alastair Swift, CEO of Willis Transport UK, echoed the experience of many: "When we got to the execution phase, we tried to do that ourselves, and that was a mistake. We hadn't been through that type of change process before, and so we needed external help. I now know that the toughest step is the execution. There is nothing fun about it, and we probably needed a lot more help than we realized." Before reviewing the typical pitfalls, first consider your own experience by completing the quiz.

How would you describe the experience of planning the implementation?

0: We did not create a plan. We just got going, and it took the time it took.

1: We had a high-level plan with sequential activities that helped us deliver in a reasonable time.

2: We had a detailed plan and tried to plan several simultaneous activities to accelerate the process.

3: We had a detailed plan, planned simultaneous activities to the extent possible, and reverse-engineered back from a challenging implementation date (e.g., 3 months in the future).

What happened to leaders from the previous organization?

0: They all stayed in place.

1: They all remained, but a few changed jobs.

2: A number changed jobs, we added some new talent, and a few previous leaders left.

3: Half stayed in their roles, around 30% changed jobs, and 20% were replaced with new talent.

How did you handle the issue of some business units or functions claiming they should be exceptions?

0: We allowed those that were most vociferous to adapt the design or time frame.

1: We tried to convince everybody and made sure that all business units or functions followed the same process.

2: We allowed some exceptions in light of management input, left them until later, and proceeded with the rest.

3: We proactively set our own objective criteria for exceptions and pushed compliance for all units that did not meet them.

How did you brief staff in the organization—people whose help you needed to design the details?

0: We relied on the communications issued to staff to date.

1: We had a few specific briefings for those whose help we needed.

2:   We gave them some standard templates to complete.

3:   We created a "cookbook" and templates for them to complete.

Once again, add up your score. If you score 10 or more, you should be feeling fairly confident. A score of 6 to 9 is fine but not great, and with 5 and below, it's clear you are reading the right chapter. It is worth reflecting on how your score here compares with your scores for the other quizzes. And if you achieved a perfect score on this quiz, please contact us to explain how you did it, as we have seldom, if ever, hit a 100 percent score for this step.

Now, let's turn to Amelia and see how she fares with her utility company reorg.

_____

After her successful final meeting on the new reorganization, Amelia realizes that a lot of work remains to be done. She meets with John, who asks her to continue running the project team until the reorganization has been delivered. It is now October, over a year in from the launch of the reorg, and John is keen to announce the new organization before the end of the year. It is some time into his tenure as CEO, and he wants to show the market and his staff that he is having an impact. Amelia and her team work hard to prepare a PowerPoint presentation that John can present to the company to tell them about the new organization.

Belatedly, Amelia and her team realize that the presentation should be run by HR. Mike, the deputy head of HR, tells them that several items in the HR presentation have significant implications under EU employment law. The presentation is therefore watered down, with some of the detail removed, and Mike launches a consultation with staff in each of the European business units who may be at risk of layoffs or having their jobs moved (as part of the centralization of trading). By contrast, Brian, the head of HR in the United States, tells Amelia: "We don't need any consultation here. We are used to making these kinds of changes and can do it very quickly." Amelia, John, and the HR team rush to get the documents ready for the HR consultation and for the company presentation. They complete them sometime in the third week of December and hold the webcasts later that week, just before the winter holiday break.

John makes his first webcast presentation in the morning (for a European audience), emphasizing the importance of the changes for the long-term success of the business. He presents well, but both he and Amelia are surprised to see that most of the questions they receive are negative and raise personal concerns about jobs. For the second webcast in the evening (for their US colleagues), Amelia and John revise the presentation to tone down the emphasis on the changes and provide more reassurance. The reaction is not so negative, but concerns about people's jobs still predominate. Just before they break for the holidays, Amelia also starts to hear rumors that some of the country managing directors are dissatisfied and may be looking at positions with competitors. Rumors from lower down in the company also suggest that some managing directors, while relaying the official line on the reorganization in public, are making it perfectly obvious through their behavior and private conversations that they have significant concerns. Amelia presents the issue to John and Mike and asks them to have individual conversations reassuring the managing directors. The managing directors' concerns lead to some further compromises in the design.

In parallel, Amelia and her team plan the detailing and launch of the new organization. They start with working out the organizational structures at the country level and updating role profiles to fit with the new approach. Next, they turn to the new role profiles required and the redesign of the capital projects process. Despite having her team of advisers from the different business units to help her, Amelia finds she has to ask so many questions of each business that it would be simpler to have the businesses complete some of the work themselves. She asks the country and function managing directors to nominate people to help, then briefs the latter on the ideas and asks them to complete the work over the next four weeks. However, it seems that these people either are too busy or do not understand the plans for the new organization as well as she thought they did. As the submissions dribble in, she notes that they are seldom in the format she has asked for; nor do they provide everything she needs.

Amelia brings up the lack of engagement to John, and with his help, she insists on a deadline of the following week. This time, the submissions just about meet her needs. However, several business leaders have changed the plans considerably. Notably, a number of them have met their cost-reduction targets in phases over the next two years rather than right away. Others have retained some "local trading activities." And still more have asked for local adaptations to the new capital projects process. The French business unit has stated that none of the changes will be possible in the next two years, because of the need for consultation with the unions.

At the same time, Amelia's team has realized just how complicated the trading centralization is going to be. First of all, they need to agree on a location. London seems the obvious one, for access to talent, commonality of language, and proximity to an existing business. But of course, all the other country managing directors oppose this. In addition, a building needs to be located and rented, new systems need to be selected and set up (at present, all local countries use different systems), and staff relocated. Some months into the process, Amelia realizes that additional resources are required to manage this part of the implementation, and she gets John's permission to set up a small team to manage it full-time.

It is now seven months into the design detailing and implementation planning, and there is still no agreement on the implementation date and many points of detail. Amelia asks John to hold a summit with the country managing directors. During a day-long meeting, they hash out the remaining details and agree, as a compromise, on a phased implementation over the next eighteen months. The easiest cost-reduction measures will be implemented first for most businesses; the new capital process will first be piloted in three regions, then rolled out after six months; the central trading organization will be set up in twelve months; and the most difficult locations will make the transition in eighteen months.

Amelia feels that, at last, the end is in sight. She and her team can start thinking about the new leaders for the trading organization and central capital projects team. The reorganization is taking an inordinately long time, distracting managers and staff from their day jobs. She also worries that some of the essential elements of the design have been lost through the various compromises. When the managing director of the French business is made the new managing director of centralized trading, Amelia finds that his criticisms change by 180 degrees: now he worries that the organization he has been given accountability for will not be effective because too many compromises have been made with the country market units.

Even if you have completed the previous three steps perfectly, step 4—detail the design and plan implementation—is always the hardest, because this is where paper plans come up against hard reality. In this step, people really have to change and difficult conversations need to be had with colleagues affected by the reorganization. It is the most complex and the most emotionally difficult step. Bizarrely, many reorgs end up launching implementation just before a major holiday, just the right time to deliver maximum depression and before a period when people have sufficient time to dust off their CVs and apply to competitors.

This step also sees the least guidance in the literature. Unfortunately, as we mentioned earlier, it is the step in which many leaders take their foot off the pedal—believing that the hard work has been completed in step 3—and delegate down to others to complete the job. If there is advice available, it usually refers to generic change-management principles, rather than the specifics of a reorganization or to how to manage the very real human impact and emotions that the change will create. Little wonder Amelia struggles more with this step than with any of the others. She valiantly addresses all the issues that come up in the best way she can. But it feels like she has lost control of the process. And of course she has. Without a comprehensive understanding of all the issues to cover, and the right sequence to cover them in, she has fallen into a number of pitfalls.

Pitfall 1: Long, Sequential Planning and Evolutionary Implementation

Most reorganizations follow the same pattern as Amelia's utility company. The reorg project team starts working on the detailing, with one thing following the other. As they progress, more and more issues surface. The work drags on. Eventually, the demands of the reorganization seem overwhelming, and someone inevitably raises the suggestion: "Should we not have a phased implementation to better manage the workload?" "Hmm," says the project sponsor, "that sounds like a good way of managing risk. It will also free up time for me to concentrate on the business." But paradoxically, the project sponsor still expects to see the business results the reorganization was supposed to deliver. The organization, depressed from dealing with a long, drawn-out implementation and facing targets it is ill equipped to deliver, cuts corners to deliver the same business results through different means. The net result of this drawn-out process is that the design detailing and implementation of half of reorganizations takes around twelve months. Two in five reorganizations underestimate the effort required to deliver this step.[1]

If we remember the points made in step 1 about value, this approach seems nonsensical: the reorganization is designed to deliver value, you realize this value only when the reorganization has been finished, and the longer you drag out the reorg, the longer the disruption and negative impact on business results. People dislike change, but they dislike uncertainty even more, and prolonged uncertainty most of all. Researchers at the University of Michigan found that persistent job insecurity can have a greater impact on ill health among workers than actual unemployment.[2] Interestingly, in one reorg we supported in Saudi Arabia, where it was clear that there would never be any job losses, the disruption and upset caused by the reorg were just as great as elsewhere in the world: although they did not have to worry about losing their jobs, workers and managers feared a loss of status. This explains why reorgs that take less than six months to complete the design detailing and implementation are more successful than those that take longer.

Yet the frequently long duration of implementation suggests that it is a rational response of sorts. Unaware of what needs to get done versus what does not, and feeling overwhelmed, leaders choose to minimize and postpone the problem. In doing so, they unwittingly cause more damage to their workforces and their businesses than they would if they had got on and implemented the change more quickly. The solution to this pitfall is conceptually simple, but requires knowledge of the full set of activities involved in this step of the reorganization:

- Start step 4 by defining the full set of activities required, prioritizing which are essential to complete now and which are nice-to-haves, unrelated to the reorg, and can be delivered later.

- Reverse-engineer the activities from your implementation date, say three months hence (or sooner if the reorg is very simple), ensuring that activities are planned in parallel, not in sequence, to achieve this. If you are completing your reorganization within the EU, there are laws in place that define the length of consultation required (see appendix C).

- Put in place two or three *immovable deadlines* in this plan so that you can seek help from the project sponsor or appropriate senior executive immediately if these deadlines start to slip, and communicate these up front.

By following these three suggestions, you get the results from the reorg quicker and minimize the time of the disruption. To help you, we have listed the typical activities required to detail the components of the reorg in table 6-1. As you will see, the majority of the work falls under people and processes. If your reorganization has only focused on the lines and boxes until now, this step is where you will really start to feel the pain. Alastair Swift, the CEO of Willis

TABLE 6-1

Typical activities required when completing step 4

Dimension	Typical activities required
People	• Reallocate leaders into new roles (at beginning of step).
	• Finalize overall head count (there may be more reductions than you need to create space for new talent).
	• Finalize the precise number of people required in each business unit or function, using a *mass balance* (the number of people by grade at the beginning versus the number at the end) to ensure that efficiency targets are met and that there is no staff or grade inflation.
	• Put a plan in place to talk individually to affected staff.
	• Run the consultation process in case of layoffs or significant changes to roles.
	• Run the nominations process for matching staff into new or changed roles (either through applications or top-down selection).
	• Arrange visas and moving packages for any international moves.
	• Update compensation (either to save cost, to standardize roles in merged departments, or to reflect the objectives of the new organization in bonus or performance pay arrangements).
	• Launch recruitment for any missing capabilities.
	• Plan training in the new ways of working.
Processes	• Realign P&L and management reporting to match the new organization.
	• Update IT systems to reflect the change (HR, finance, sales, logistics, procurement, etc.).
	• Redesign management and operational processes, testing and refining them and communicating those changes.
Structure	• Finalize reporting lines down to the front line in each business unit or function, including any adaptation for local conditions.
	• Standardize job titles or job families.
	• Confirm or adjust job grading.
	• Complete new role profiles or job descriptions, including targets.

Transport UK, told us: "We should have pushed a lot harder to build the systems before we launched what we were trying to do. Without these systems to support it, we had no way of proving success or failure of the organization that we were putting in place that would resonate with anybody. We pushed faster than we had the capability, hoping that the systems would catch up, and they didn't."

At this point, we'd like to highlight the importance of changing the P&L and management reporting, because so many reorgs fail to do this and get left with a car without a steering wheel. You've given it a great engine and you hope it's going in the right direction, but you have no way of knowing. If you have made a meaningful organizational change (rather than just shifted around the senior management deck chairs), you will need a different P&L roll-up, different key performance indicators, and different handovers or service-level agreements between the constituent parts of the organization. You will need to split out the P&L, decide who is responsible for what, who can decide on what, and how to quickly get that into new reporting. This will be likely to require IT systems changes to manage the roll-up efficiently, and the design and testing of these changes should be prioritized as early as possible in this step. These considerations can also shape the design. In regulated businesses (like utilities and banks), you need to be careful about which costs are added to the regulated parts of the business, versus those added to the unregulated parts. And if your company is multinational, different countries' tax systems and incentives can also shape where you site activities (although you should, obviously, stick to the letter and spirit of the laws to avoid incurring regulatory wrath and public uproar, as some technology companies have found). All in all, the critical interlinkage between the new organization and the P&L is one reason why it is important to have a finance professional on your reorg project team.

A second major issue that needs careful planning and sequencing in the plumbing and wiring of your reorg is the nominations of people for new jobs. Clearly, you need to have worked out the detailed org charts before you put people into them. Indeed, in the

European Union, labor law often prevents putting people in new jobs before you have formalized the new structure (see appendix C). The same can be true for mergers. In addition, you also need to have worked out the number of people, by grade, for each unit of the organization before and after the change, to avoid staff and grade inflation and to confirm that you have made the savings you intended, if this is one of the reasons behind your reorg. One helpful approach is to create a series of simple mass-balance charts that show, by department, the number of positions by grade at the beginning of the reorg, the number moved to other departments, the number removed, the number of new roles added, and the end position. See figure 6-1 for an example. This chart shows that forty-two positions have been transferred to another department—these do not count as savings. A whole management level of the organization has then been removed (constituting twenty-one positions). Seventy-seven positions have then been removed due to frontline efficiencies. Finally, thirteen positions have been added back to improve management control and make the management spans of control (number of reports per manager) work. Note that the chart enables you to compare numbers of people before and after the reorg—to guard against unconscious grade inflation (something we often see). It is important to be rigorous in counting actual people and not allow phony savings from managers declaring unfilled job vacancies (of which there may be many) as savings. Having defined the number of positions required, using the mass balance approach, you can finally move on to nominating people for roles. Again, unless you plan this rigorously and get the activities in the right order, you will find that your implementation drags out.

Now, when companies get to the nomination process itself, what typically happens is that all the leaders get together in a room and decide which staff they are going to send where (often because the clock has timed out and they are already behind). Now, this rapid-fire approach can sometimes be the right answer. However,

FIGURE 6-1

Illustrative mass balance

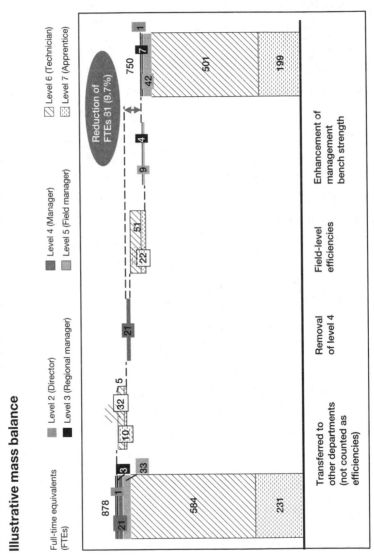

you should consider running an application process whereby staff can apply for jobs through HR. That way, you can get people applying for a position out of genuine interest rather than because they are told to. Of course, the voluntary approach requires good planning so that you can complete the previous tasks and still have time to manage an application process.

You should also consider standardizing job titles through the reorg. Many companies—especially those that have been put together by a series of mergers—have developed a multiplicity of job titles and responsibilities. This variety causes unnecessary complexity in the organization and makes it difficult to manage moves, plan career paths, and design training programs. The reorg is an opportunity to address these issues.

Broadening out to the full set of plumbing and wiring activities laid out in table 6-2, Neil Hayward, group people director of the UK Post Office, sums this up nicely: "Don't start implementation until the detailed implementation plan is clear and has been agreed on by the whole executive team. And part of that plan has to be real commitment by the leadership to spend time supporting the transition and providing counsel to those in their teams who are affected by the change." Figure 6-2 provides an illustration of such a plan.

Pitfall 2: Leaving Leaders in Old Positions to Resist Change

One of the biggest mistakes in any reorganization is to leave leaders in their existing positions and to allow the reorg to be portrayed as something separate, *happening to* the organization. This attitude often leads to resistance, as leaders seek to minimize the impact on their part of the organization. In this situation, the reorganization sponsor and project team seem to be the only people pushing the

FIGURE 6-2

Sample work plan

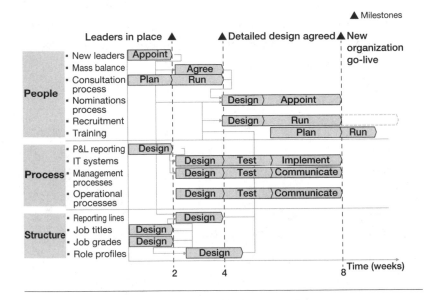

reorg. It saps their energy as they encounter resistance from all sides. Of course, when leadership changes are made at the end of this step, many of those leaders who have been resisting find that they are now in charge of new units that are half-baked, precisely because of their own resistance (as seen in the example of the French managing director changing roles). If you have ever been in this position, you will no doubt recognize many of the challenges that Amelia encountered. Probably, you have seen worse.

The solution to this pitfall is simple: give leaders a stake in the new organization sooner—ideally at the end of step 3 or the start of step 4. And when you do this, consider moving some of the leaders who are most resistant to the change out of their existing roles and into some of the very new roles. You will be amazed how quickly views change when people switch roles! For example, an energy company did this when it was moving from a geographic model (all its assets managed by geographic location) to a functional model (every functional team is an asset reporting to a central functional department). Some of the most vociferous regional leaders suddenly found themselves moved into functional roles and stopped resisting the change. The rest of the organization really noticed this change of mood and became more positive.

Moving leaders early leads to some complexity, as leaders are expected to manage their existing roles while planning for their new ones. But this is why we pay leaders the big bucks. Better to load the complexity onto them than force hundreds or thousands of people in the business to endure it. Imagine how the story above might have played out differently had the obstructive French managing director realized that he would be the new leader of the trading organization from the beginning, or had the US managing director realized that he would be asked to lead the new central capital projects team across all locations.

Of course, taking these actions early may reveal that some of the current leaders do not like their roles in the new organization. But it is better to surface this early, rather than wait for years of resistance before addressing the problem. Occasionally, some leaders who were very successful in the old organization may not be not the right people to lead the new one. This situation is unfortunate, but if this is the case, you and they need to part company now. To illustrate this, here is a conversation between one of us and a new executive at a client:

> *Me:* So, why did you decide to join this firm?

> *Executive:* Well, your consulting firm designed a new organization for my old company, and it became clear that I no longer had a meaningful role.

Me (concerned): Oh . . . Did you disagree with the reorganization then?

Executive: No, it made sense to me. And it was probably right for the company. It was simply that the kind of role I wanted to do no longer existed in the organization. So, I knew I needed to change firms.

Not all executives are quite so self-perceptive (or understanding). Many go down fighting. So, sometimes, the project sponsor or another responsible executive needs to make the decision for them. Conversely, you need to identify the leaders who are going to be successful in the new model, reassure them of their future, and make sure you keep them. This informal process of taking the most critical talent in the organization out for a cup of tea (or a beer or whatever) and telling them how valued they are is often ignored at this stage in the process, but it can significantly reduce talent loss. Even though it is deliberately informal, this process needs to be coordinated so that you do not miss key people. Left in doubt, any high-talent employees you miss will be the ones dusting off their CVs to send to your competitors.

Any rule of thumb is simply that. But this one is good to consider: change 20 percent of leaders, move 30 percent, and keep half in place. For the parts of the organization that are changing (remember, it may not be the whole organization), compare your plans with this rule. The exact proportions may differ, but if you find that you are leaving almost 100 percent of the leaders in place, you are probably falling into this pitfall.

Rob Rosenberg of DHL described the reason why he and his colleagues made leadership changes before implementing their reorg: "You have to have a few pioneers who are willing to make the new roles work. Some of the moves we made were controversial, but by putting very senior and respected leaders in new roles, we demonstrated how serious we were about changing how the organization worked." In another interview, Lawrence Gosden of Thames Water extolled the virtues of changing leaders—in his case by bringing in new leaders from outside the company: "It takes time to change leaders' behaviors, so, if you want to drive a new way of thinking, find the industry that excels in what you want and bring in someone from there as a seed and a shortcut. You can grow and mature leaders into a new mind-set, but this takes time and, in a reorg, you do not usually have that luxury."

Pitfall 3: Trying to Change Everything, and Changing Nothing

There will always be some valid exceptions to the changes you propose. The most obvious one is where a particular organizational unit, such as country business unit, is subscale (i.e., not large enough in terms of revenues/profits or simply activities), and splitting it into different parts of the organization would lead to inefficiencies. In some countries, employment legislation or union agreements may make changes very difficult and time-consuming. And in some business areas, there may be legitimate reasons to take a different approach (though be very careful of this one, as everyone will claim it). Of course, there are also many invalid exceptions. In table 6-2, we have laid out some that we have heard over the years and the appropriate responses.

You will no doubt hear more objections or excuses. Let us know what they are. Remember that a lot of the objections will be attempts to delay or undermine your plans. Keep faith with your ideas, and attune your ear to exceptions that are not really valid.

TABLE 6-2

Some common excuses for not participating in a reorg

Invalid exception	Appropriate response
Regulatory or safety rules do not allow this.	Show me the precise wording of these regulations.
Legal or financial requirements demand that I have this role or arrangement (e.g., a country CEO, a local CFO, a separate company).	Show me the law that says this. [And if there is such a law or requirement:] We can meet these requirements by having someone who holds this role for external purposes. It does not need to shape the way we organize internally.
We do not have the people in place to fill the positions that are required.	Let HR know which positions we need to fill, and we will work to fill them.
I need to keep Bob/Cindy happy and cannot change his/her role.	Why are Bob/Cindy so crucial? Is he/she crucial enough to change the design? Have we spoken to Bob/Cindy about alternative roles and opportunities?
I have just changed my part of the organization; I cannot change it again.	The whole organization needs to change to minimize the complexity. If you do not change now, you will create uncertainty, because your organization will know that future change (to align with the rest of the organization) will be required.
We cannot change until the new IT system is in place.	Better to change the way of working and have the IT system fit that than the reverse.
A staged or evolutionary approach will work better for my part of the organization.	This will drag out the uncertainty, which people dislike more than change. It is better to get the change over and done with.

Having dealt with the requests for inappropriate exceptions, you are left with a minority of cases that are legitimate exceptions. At this stage, it is important to remember that you should *treat your reorganization like any other business problem*. So, the aim is to deliver value, not to drive conformity for conformity's sake. You should try to ensure that of all the changes that you envisaged, you can deliver at least 80 percent of them as soon as possible. To reach this goal, you can either achieve over 80 percent of the savings as soon as possible or change the business units that make up more than 80 percent of the revenues and profits as soon as possible. With this 80 percent, you should make sure that you detail the 100 percent of how the organization will run in the future (laying out the processes, planning the people moves, specifying the structure of the front line). This is not the time for high-level principles.

For the parts of the organization that do not change yet, set some later deadlines or trigger points for changes (where it makes sense). For example, Amelia could allow the French market unit to implement the same changes six months later, when it has dealt with a particular customer issue, or the Eastern European market unit could be allowed to implement the changes when it reaches a certain size of revenues. After you have set the later deadlines, you then need to monitor delivery. But in the meantime, don't let these exceptions hold you back from delivering the value you need, as soon as possible.

Pitfall 4: Confusing Your People

As Amelia realizes in our story, there comes a point when a central HQ team, however well briefed, cannot deliver the details required and needs to ask the business for help. However, the people who have been asked to help will not have been involved in the weeks or months of febrile discussions leading to this point and are likely to be confused by all the jargon you now spring on them. Elon Musk told us: "Communication is fundamental to productivity. So people should be wary of code names or acronyms. If someone is making a presentation and starts using acronyms, I ask them what the acronyms mean. In my experience, half the time they do not know." If you don't take time to explain exactly what you mean, don't be surprised if you don't get the input that you need.

In addition, this phase of widening involvement in the reorg will obviously lead to wider discussion on the details. If this discussion is not fully informed, confusion and worry might spread throughout your company. This situation can worsen if you have left disruptive leaders in place. Hannah Meadley-Roberts of the European Bank of Reconstruction and Development, previously a senior civil servant in the UK Ministry of Justice, told us: "The one thing you must have is management speaking with one voice. If staff see any gaps between leaders, it makes things very difficult." This is exactly the situation in which business results start to worsen.

We will not mislead you: there will always be some distraction and confusion at this stage. But you can help yourself by setting out very clearly what you want to do and why; what input you need from the business; what this input should look like; which decisions are set in stone and which are open to refinement or improvement; and when you need their input. With this cookbook approach, you can improve the process considerably.

. . .

The following cases illustrate ways to address the pitfalls we've just described.

Winning Way 1: Plan in Parallel, Implement as a Revolution

An executive in charge of one of the global business units of a leading industrial service company was in the midst of a reorganization. This company had a leading reputation for R&D and providing high-value services, but its industry was in the middle of a deep commodity price fall. The business unit in question actually covered two business segments: one, a higher-value, high-tech segment, which had always been the focus and which brought in much higher margins, and the second, a lower-margin, more operational business segment, which had always been something of a second fiddle. In the context of a crashing market, the first, higher-value segment was suffering most, whereas the second market was proving much more robust. Yet local operations managers in each of the locations still favored the high-value market (where they had much more experience) and were struggling to defend that while growing an unfamiliar market.

For the executive in charge, the organizational barriers to growth in the lower-margin, higher-growth business provided a strong argument for a reorg and she had already set up a project team. In fact, this was just the sort of situation that required a top-down reorganization rather than bottom-up tinkering (see the discussion on this in chapter 5). Timing was very tight. The new organization needed to be launched within three months, in time for the start of the financial year in April. Meanwhile, commodity prices continued to fall, first by a half and then by 80 percent. The company's clients were suffering, and they were passing on the pain to the service company through "haircuts" to prices. This only served to reinforce the need for rapid reorganization.

The value at stake had been quantified and agreed on with the CEO (step 1). The business unit needed to defend as much as possible its leading position in one high-value but rapidly shrinking business segment while, at the same time, shifting its focus to a more robust business segment with much lower-cost, lower-tech offerings. The strengths and weaknesses of the organization were also clear (step 2): the business unit had a sterling reputation for quality and technological innovation—essential in the high-value business segment—but it also needed to develop a lean and mean operating model to compete against lower-cost operators in the lower-cost segment. Such an operating model would be a counter-cultural approach for the company.

The broad outlines of the new organization had already been defined (step 3). The business unit was due to merge with another lower-cost operation with complementary skills and would be split in two in each major geographic area. One operational manager would continue to cover the shrinking high-value segment, and another would cover the growing lower-value one. This approach reflected the fact that the two segments required different services and different ways of operating and were run by different managers on the customer side.

All this notwithstanding, step 4 was proving challenging. The business unit was not short of talent and ideas. Its leaders had launched a number of activities. But the executive in charge needed to know which activities were essential to complete now and which could be left until later. She worried that without experience in running a successful reorg, her talented team were running in all directions, often overlapping, and were not necessarily driving toward the results she needed.

We were called in to help, with the assistance of one analyst to provide support in analysis and planning. The first step was to define all the activities required, to sequence them in time to deliver within the three months, and to ensure that each activity had a leader responsible for it. In contrast to most reorganizations we have encountered in this step (where typically a large number of activities are not being completed), the leaders of the business unit were covering all of the activities required—and many more! For example, they were planning to address a number of long-standing anomalies in operational standards and IT systems at the same time that they were conducting the reorg. Therefore the first thing we did was to hold a meeting of the leadership team to agree on the plan. We decided on which activities we absolutely needed to do now, which were nice-to-haves, and which should be postponed to prevent the reorg being delayed. We also worked to ensure clear accountabilities that did not overlap.

We sequenced the activities working back from the outcome needed in three months' time. Three things became clear from this exercise. First, the detail of the organizational structures and the exact number of positions for each region needed to be defined early to allow sufficient time to nominate people and obtain visas, if necessary, to get these people in place. Second, the leadership needed time to think about how to handle the people consequences of the change (including training managers on having difficult but honest discussions and supporting individuals who would leave the company). Finally, the IT changes necessary to allow the P&L to be managed and systems to be accessed from day one required careful planning—including when they would go offline for testing. To determine which countries needed to be reorganized, we also needed to establish some clear rules for exceptions based on the share of revenues across both segments: if a country had sizable volumes of revenues from both segments, it would split; if one or both segments were subpar, it would not.

We then analyzed the revenues for both segments, together with the number of operational trips to the customer for each segment (reflecting that the revenues from the high-value segment could be large but the number of operational trips could be small). We established cutoffs for both revenues and the number of operational trips above which a country could be regarded as being above critical mass, if both business segments were present: in these cases, the countries would be reorganized. Below these cutoffs, splitting the business into two would make no operational sense and would lead to inefficiencies. In yet another illustration of the Pareto principle, the countries that would not split accounted for less than 20 percent of both revenues and earnings before tax.

Through the following eleven weeks, we held weekly management meetings with the leadership team to ensure that progress was being made. Inevitably, there were challenges along the way, as there always are. At one stage, progress in a couple of critical areas fell behind by a week and a half and the team had to take accelerated action to get these areas back on track. Occasionally, the senior leadership had to intervene personally to talk to individuals affected by the reorg or who were at risk of being demotivated by the changes. Through careful monitoring, however, the need for these interventions was identified in good time, and although some discussions were difficult, employee retention was very good. By the end of March, we were able to appoint operations managers for both high-value and low-cost segments for every country and had 95 percent of them in place (the remainder were awaiting visas).

At the operational level (the people delivering the services at the customer site), we decided that around 40 percent of the countries (by revenue) would be ready to split in March, but around 40 percent by revenue would have to wait until June (mainly to ensure that the customers were happy with the move and to address logistical challenges where sites were scattered across a country). While this broke our rule for revolutionary change in one step to accelerate value and minimize disruption, sometimes you have to break a rule to suit reality. Nevertheless, the implementation was fully completed in less than six months, far quicker than the vast majority of reorganizations.

Winning Way 2: Give Leaders a Stake
in the New Organization

Returning to the water utility case from the previous chapter, which has now reached the stage of design detailing and implementation planning. The reorganization had also expanded beyond field operations, with significant changes also envisaged in the way the company planned and scheduled its operational work for plant and infrastructure. In short, the company was changing from a business split between clean water and wastewater to one divided up into planners, schedulers, and doers, across both clean water and wastewater. Obviously, this change in organization demanded a very different way of operating and required different skills of the company's leaders.

To give leaders a stake in the new organization and prevent them from seeing the reorg as something happening to them, very early in the process the leaders were notified of their new roles. For example, the leader previously responsible for planning, scheduling, and doing operational work in one region was no longer responsible for planning and scheduling work, only for doing that work, albeit across a greater area. This early inclusion gave the leaders a stake in setting up the new organization and an impetus to reach agreement on it quickly (as this would minimize the time during which they had to be responsible for two roles—their old one and their new one). It also demystified the process for staff to some degree: rather than thinking that they might be reporting to some unknown head of water treatment operations, they now knew, for example, that they would be reporting to Marie.

Of course, the early involvement of leaders did not eliminate all the problems of the reorganization. Changes to people's pay and conditions still caused alarm. And some areas of the business were more difficult than others to split into "plan, schedule, and do"—notably the teams responding to water pipe leaks and sewer flooding—because of the complexity of their activities and the significant impact on the regulatory evaluation of the company. It was important to get the reorg in these areas right, and here we conducted detailed analysis of the process and different activities.

The appointment of leaders into their new positions early in the process also had another benefit. It enabled us to conduct dry runs of the performance management discussions that would follow the reorganization, so that leaders could understand what was required of them. For the dry runs, we continued to run the regular weekly performance management reviews with leaders in their existing positions. Then, immediately afterward, we ran another performance management review with the same (real) data. In this second review, the leaders were able to practice their new roles before the D-day of the new organization.

The first time we held one of these dry runs, it was a disaster! Rather than sticking to their new roles (focusing only on planning, scheduling, or doing), the leaders, used to having all three of these responsibilities, started ranging into the responsibilities of their peers. Clearly, there was a lot of learning required before they could focus only on their own new area and trust their peers to exercise good judgment in theirs. The second time we ran the dry run, the experience was better. The third time, better still. By the time D-day arrived, the leaders were ready.

Of course, when we say the first dry run was a disaster, we really mean it was a great success—identifying the areas where leaders needed to develop their skills and prepare for their new roles. Far better that this happened as a dry run instead of at the first performance management meeting of the new organization. But of course, the latter situation is exactly what happens in most reorgs: with limited preparation, leaders are parachuted into their new roles and left to work out the details by experimenting with real-life performance.

Winning Way 3: Identify the 80 Percent to Change, Do That in 100 Percent Detail

In our work with a global retailer, we saw a good example of this 80–100 approach. Having conducted all three steps from the previous chapters, the retailer decided that it was going to slim down its regions very substantially to reduce duplication between its country structures and the management layers above. It also wanted to put in place new processes for performance management, store event management, and innovation.

The CEO called a meeting of her executive team to discuss the implementation of these changes. All her team members were supportive—except for the head of Asia. His concern in removing the Asian region was that the business was subscale there (so countries were not big enough to support themselves), his talent in Asia was quite poor at the country level, and he was in the middle of a major store transformation program. He therefore requested that the changes should be rolled out to Asia one year later than to the rest of the company.

His request for a delayed schedule was debated in substantial detail, but the team eventually concluded that this was a fair challenge and that Asia would be granted an exception. They determined that the difference in Asia's organization would have relatively little effect on the rest of the group for that year. They also decided that even though its structure would not change, Asia would still have to change its performance management and event management processes at the same time as the rest of the group.

Having decided on the 80 percent of the organization to which the changes should apply, the team then went on to detail all of the changes in depth before implementation (the 100 percent). Detailing the changes included, for example, laying out the full annual calendar for the new product development process, showing who needed to make what decisions and when.

Although we did not deliver a full "decision-rights framework," in our experience these frameworks are not especially helpful.[3] Although they detail who has a whole range of rights in decision making, ranging from the minor input to the more major decisions, they create huge rule books, which are impossible to follow in real life (in fact, few people ever take them out of the drawer again). Instead, the important thing is to focus on who is responsible for making each decision at each step. This process was then tested in a workshop where the participants role-played each step in the full annual calendar. The exercise revealed numerous issues that were corrected before the final process was documented. The team also spent some time working on the communications around the change to make it clear why it was right for Asia to be an exception.

The CEO was disappointed that the whole organization could not move together, but there was little loss of value in delaying Asia (the smallest part of the structure) and she could see the risk in changing Asia while it was transforming its stores. The implementation of the process in the rest of the company, however, went through successfully and on time.

Winning Way 4: Create the Cookbook

When we worked with a global logistics player that had gone through steps 1, 2, and 3, we (and they) faced a tough issue on step 4: the organization was so large that there was a danger that a centrally implemented change would fail to accommodate the needs of the different parts of the business. So, instead it was decided that the plan would be central, but that the implementation would be local.

To support this decision, we decided, together with the organization, that three documents were needed: (1) a description of what the organization should broadly look like when complete; (2) a methodology for how to create the precise answer for any part of the business; and (3) a plan for how to roll out the methodology to over one hundred locations.

The team that had undertaken steps 1, 2, and 3 created these three documents. The first document, the description of the organization, detailed what an ideal country- and site-level structure should look like (in terms of people, processes, and structure) when the change was complete. This description had variants for small and large countries and small and large sites and was clear about the elements that were fixed and those that could be varied locally.

The second document described the process that should be used in each country or site to take it from today's organization to the future organization. This document was, in effect, a very streamlined version of steps 1, 2, and 3 but at a local level (not as much is needed as the overall answer is already decided).

The third document described the rollout plan. It detailed which countries and sites would be transformed by when—and thus when the value would be delivered.

Together, these documents formed a cookbook that would enable managers in the local businesses to deliver the plumbing and wiring of the reorg.

. . .

Having absorbed the lessons of these case examples, let's rerun step 4 for Amelia and John's company and see how the step might play out differently—that is, play out better.

After her successful final meeting on the new reorganization, Amelia realizes that a lot of work remains to be done. She meets with John, who asks her to continue her work running the project team until the reorganization has been delivered. John and Amelia both agree that they need to review all the work that must be done, create a plan for accelerated implementation, and align the leadership team behind it.

Amelia spends the next week in conclave with her team from across the business. They identify all the areas of work to complete under the themes of people, process, and structure. She quickly realizes that significant IT changes are required and that she will need much more help from HR to manage the design of new role profiles, the selection of people into these roles, and the necessary layoffs. Clearly, step 4 is going to require more horsepower than the previous steps. She therefore asks John to transfer an IT business partner and an HR representative into her team.

After the plan has been completed and signed off by the CEO, he and Amelia hold a confidential meeting to plan the appointment of leaders into the pivotal new roles. They decide to reduce senior head count (which can be achieved through two forthcoming retirements), to merge some of the smaller country market units under one managing director, and to move some of the managing directors into the new functional roles. They decide to make the North American managing director the head of the central capital projects team, and the managing director of the French business the new head of trading. When John informs these two leaders of their new roles, their reactions are something of a shock. The North American managing director tells John that he is only really interested in running a US business and does not want a global role. They therefore agree to manage his exit, and John hands over to HR the task of finding a replacement and putting together a package for him. While this news is unwelcome, John is glad that they have identified this issue early. Meanwhile, the former French managing director, who has a passion for trading, takes on his new role with enthusiasm, driving it forward personally and thereby easing the pressure on Amelia. With his eye on the future, he also becomes more flexible on making changes to the French business. Of course, there are regulatory and union challenges, but in most cases, it is possible to achieve the reorg's objectives.

The following week, John and Amelia stage a full meeting of the leadership team. By now the team is used to this pattern of decision making, and absenteeism has ended: they see that the new organization is going to happen. Amelia—with John's agreement—has defined a set revenue and operational criteria that delineate which businesses must change and which can be allowed as exceptions. Only the new Eastern European and Asian businesses are accepted as exceptions that do not need to change. France is accepted as a temporary exception, but even if the timetable is slower, the business still needs to change. John also sets three immovable deadlines: the first for country input into local organizational structures, process adaptations, and final head-count targets; the second for nominations of leaders (below the level of the managing directors) into new roles; and the third for nominations of other staff into new roles (especially into the new centralized trading business). To help the country teams, Amelia promises to send them a cookbook within one week, outlining exactly what they need to do, with templates for their input. Meanwhile, Amelia and her central team run the layoff process, IT changes, and process redesign centrally, as there is no reason why these processes should be different across the different locations.

Only after the leadership meeting has agreed on the plan do Amelia and John prepare a communication to the rest of the business. This takes the form of two webcasts: one in the morning, European time, for Europe and Asia and another in the afternoon for North America. In these webcasts, John reminds staff of the business rationale for the reorganization, the broad plans for how the new organization will work, and the dates by which staff will know more. While a number of questions show that staff are still worried about their jobs, the clarity on when things are happening provides some reassurance. Moreover, John and Amelia, having briefed the managing directors in advance, are confident that these leaders are well placed to follow up on any questions locally.

Despite some inevitable slippages in deadlines and variability in the quality of input from a few localities, Amelia, drawing on encouragement from the CEO, marshals all the work she needs in time for D-day, four months after the start of step 4. France is going to follow three months later. And Eastern Europe and Asia will only reorganize after they reach a certain critical mass of revenues. But 85 percent of the organization (by revenues) will reorganize on D-day. Surely, now, Amelia's mission is complete?

How to Handle Communications in Step 4

- **Staff and leadership needs:** For staff, this step, rather than the previous one, is critical. This is the step in which staff members learn what their new jobs will be and, perhaps for a minority of them, whether they will need to find work elsewhere. Those who leave need to know the terms and how they will be supported through the process. Those who remain will finally be prepared to listen to stories about the exciting new world of the reorg. Leaders should have learned their future in the previous step or early in this one. However, they too have needs in this step. It will often be down to these leaders to explain the new arrangements in the organization.

- **What to communicate:** Near the beginning of this step, you should communicate which positions in the organization are to be affected and how you will determine this. Indeed, within the EU, depending on the scale of the changes, you may be legally obliged to run a period of consultation, which may have started even earlier (see appendix C). You should provide leaders with the communications material they need to inform their staff. Finally, when staff are ready to take their roles, that is the time for exciting and engaging them.

- **How to communicate:** If you are entering a consultation period, then you will need to communicate broadly and effectively. Depending on your jurisdiction, there may be legal requirements around how you consult on changes (see appendix C), so it is important to ensure that your HR reorg team member is intimately involved in the decisions and that you seek legal advice where necessary. It can be helpful to use a variety of communication approaches, including a town hall, e-mail, and cascade briefings through managers. Typically, this step requires more people to get involved in leading communications. Until now the communicators have largely been the CEO or leader of the organizational unit in question, and other key leaders. Now, communications should be initiated by a much wider set of managers. You need to provide time for leaders and managers to rehearse messages and prepare for tricky questions and situations. They need to get comfortable with the messages before they can be effective communicators to their teams. If the reorg is being done right, there will be changes to people and processes as well as to reporting lines, so the messages can be quite complex. For example, we once ran a workshop for a pharma company where the top hundred or so managers got together for a day to talk through how to engage their staff and explain what was happening and then to practice in small groups dealing with tough situations. They looked at questions like, If a high performer who is worried about his or her job asks if it is safe, what can you say? Legal and HR managers were present in those breakouts to provide coaching and support and to make sure that no one broke the legal rules of consultation. Investing this kind of time is invaluable in ensuring that people get clear and consistent answers about what is going on. When people are ready to move into their new roles, you can launch a much more exciting set of communications about the future, because people will then (finally) be ready to listen. You can still communicate using traditional methods such as speeches, e-mails, and posters, but you should also consider some more-novel approaches such as viral videos where workers explain what has changed in the way they do their jobs. In this step more than any other, it is critical to monitor the results of communications and act on any feedback quickly.

Step 4 Summary

Pitfalls

- Long, sequential planning and evolutionary implementation

- Leaving leaders in old positions to resist change

- Trying to change everything, or changing nothing

- Confusing your people

Winning Ways

- Plan in parallel, implement as a revolution

- Give leaders a stake in the new organization

- Identify the 80% to change, do that in 100% detail

- Create the cookbook

How to Use These Ideas in Your Organization

- Start this step by reviewing all the activities needed to deliver the new organization and the value it was designed for. Use the template/checklist in this chapter.

- Decide how you want to implement the changes: e.g., layer by layer, function by function, or all at once.

- Make sure that all the necessary activities are included and that all nice-to-have activities are excluded (you will be plenty busy without adding nonessential tasks!).

- Reverse-engineer the plan of activities to deliver your new organization in three to four months (or less if your reorg is simpler). Make sure you involve HR at the earliest stage.

- Set two or three immovable deadlines to plan these activities around, agree on these with the leadership team up front, and communicate immediately to the reorg project sponsor or appropriate senior executive as soon as there are any slippages.

- Address issues with leaders *now*. Do not be nostalgic. Just because someone was successful in the old organization does not mean that they will be successful in the new one. Use the rule of thumb "Change 20 percent of leaders, move 30 percent, and retain half of leaders in place" to judge how you are doing (although every organization is different). This rule of thumb is very difficult to follow as it affects real people and their jobs. But the reorganization will only be successful if you have the right people in the right roles. Only communicate to the wider organization after aligning your leaders.

- Set some objective measures for which parts of the organization can be exceptions to the change, using business criteria (ideally around financial or operational metrics). On the one hand, remember that the reorganization is designed to meet business needs (do not push conformity for conformity's sake, as it may lead to inefficiencies). On the other hand, do not accept exceptions based on opinions.

- Identify the activities that need to be delivered by the business units or functions themselves (especially around organizational structure and numbers of people). Get them involved early, and support them through the methodology. Also identify the activities that are best done centrally (especially around people moves, processes, and IT systems).

7

Step 5

Launch, Learn, and Course-Correct

You have implemented the reorganization: the work is done, right? Well, consider the advice from earlier in the book: *treat your reorganization like any other business problem.* If you think of reorganization as a business tool, you will only be finished when you see the business results you wanted. So, now is the time to confirm that the reorg is delivering what you expected and to make the necessary course corrections if it is not. Consider the quiz below for your current reorganization or a past one.

How do you judge the results of your reorganization?

0: We trusted in the leaders of the reorganization.

1: We set criteria for whether each business unit and function has fully reorganized, and we monitor against this.

2: We measured the detailed inputs of the reorganization (e.g., new capital process in place, increased sales calls, operational uptime).

3: We measured both the inputs and the business outputs of the reorganization (e.g., improved capital efficiency, sales performance, operational costs).

After the reorganization, what was your advice to the business?

0: We told them to put the reorg behind them; it's time to get back to business as usual.

1: We told the staff that they needed to work in some specific, different ways.

2: We reemphasized the business rationale for the reorg and held people accountable for delivery.

3: We launched business improvement initiatives to capture the value we wanted.

How did you identify and respond to issues in the new organization?

0: We were confident that we made the right choice on the organizational design, so we regarded any issues as teething problems.

1: If any issues came up, we dealt with them as soon as possible.

2: We had a formal process for communicating issues up through the chain of command.

3: We had a process for communicating issues up through the chain of command, and we ran a formal check (5,000-mile check) after implementation.

How do you capture the lessons from your reorganization?

0: We never do this.

1: We keep a record of people who have been involved in the reorg, so that we know whom to call on next time.

2: We have a formal process for capturing lessons learned from the reorg.

3: We track the business outputs of all our reorgs, compare these with the actions we took, and learn the lessons for the future.

Now add up your score. Our experience is that this is the least thought-through step in a reorg. So, if you scored above 9, please get in touch with us and share your experiences. If below 5, you are failing to extract the maximum value from your reorganization.

Let's see how a typical post-implementation experience would play out by returning one last time to our utility company example.

After a week of late nights, finalizing a number of difficult, last-minute management moves, and ensuring that everything was in place for the reorganization, Amelia is again clearing her desk to return to her day job. D-day for the reorganization has passed, and the concerns of the naysayers failed to materialize. With the exception of a dozen people awaiting visas to move to the new trading center in London, all roles have been filled. The recently realigned systems all work. The layoffs, while painful, had been executed fairly and quickly. Operational performance has been relatively unaffected. Amelia breathes a sigh of relief. It has not been easy, but she has come through it, and there is every sign that the reorg has been a success.

In their final weekly meeting, John thanks her for her and her team's efforts. Her reorg team, which grew to a dozen full-time members, acquitted itself well; all the members have found rewarding positions in the new organization. Amelia, conscientious as ever, has put together a handover document for John's chief of staff. In it, she has defined several criteria to confirm that the new organization has been implemented effectively in all locations. She has defined a timeline for the French business to complete its transition. And she has set criteria by which to judge the critical mass of the new businesses (Eastern Europe and Asia) and high-level ideas and a plan for their transition, drawn from her experience.

In the first week of the new organization, John again holds two webcasts for the entire firm. He acknowledges that the past few months have been a difficult time: a number of valued colleagues have exited the business, and, like him, others have had to move with their families to new locations—often new countries. He thanks staff for their patience and reminds them why this was all necessary: the business needed to shed costs to be able to compete. Now, he hopes, with the future of the business secured, they can deliver the results their shareholders expect, outperform the opposition, and create a truly great environment for people to work in. He concludes by telling them that the reorg is over. Now is the time to get back to business as usual.

Some months later . . . Amelia is enjoying her position as a senior member of the new central capital projects function. Using her knowledge of frontline work and connections across the organization, she is making sure the governance process the team is putting in place is practical and nonbureaucratic and reflects the needs of the market units. She has received a few calls from the CEO's chief of staff over the past few months (with regard to getting the P&L and transfer price for trading right and ensuring that proposals from the French business meet the original intent of the reorganization). But now she receives a call from John himself. He tells her that some festering issues have risen to his attention. The interface between plant operations and trading is not working well—and each side is blaming the other. Financial results from a few businesses do not meet the opex targets that had been set initially. Safety performance has not improved. And local capital project managers are unsure about whom to look to when they need to get permission to change or adapt a standard for their project.

Amelia and a few relevant members of her original team are pulled out of their day jobs for a month to address these issues. The technical solutions are not hard to reach. What takes time is resetting the relationships that had grown confrontational while the problems had been allowed to fester. Several times, she needs to call on John's help for a quiet word with senior managers involved in the dispute. With regard to the businesses failing to achieve their cost-reduction targets, it transpires that other costs, unrelated to the reorganization, have hurt the picture. Without the reorg, the position would have been worse. Amelia concludes that the reorganization can still be regarded as a success, although some of the managers involved in the disputes have developed a different impression, which will take time to shift.

After the intervention, Amelia and John meet up to discuss the lessons of the reorganization. Both of them agree that while the reorganization was clearly worthwhile, they do not want to see another large reorganization of the company anytime soon, given the pain involved. At the same time, they realize that their industry is continuing to transform itself, with regulatory changes relating to climate change and new, fast-moving entrants focused on only parts of the business. They conclude that other, smaller organizational changes to different parts of the business will most likely be required. Amelia therefore completes a register of all those actively involved in the reorg, to be held by the vice president of HR, so that local leaders will know whom to come to for help should they need to reorganize. That done, Amelia and John call an end to the reorganization and return to their day jobs. It is just over eighteen months since they launched it.

John and Amelia have coped as well as possible in situations where they lacked the experience and structure to plan. But if you have read the rest of this book, you will no doubt be unsurprised to know that their actions were far from perfect and that they fell into a number of pitfalls. We explain these below.

Pitfall 1: Only Measuring Inputs

Something happens during a reorganization: the effort required is so extraordinary that the reorg becomes an end in itself. Little wonder that, at the end of the process, the original business rationale for the reorg is often forgotten. In many cases, the reorg has taken so long that other, unrelated initiatives have been launched to achieve the same ends. This leads to the frequent (but not very helpful) question that we referred to above: will the improved performance come from the reorg or from other initiatives?

In this context, most executives end up measuring the success of the reorganization by looking at inputs. These can be whether elements of the organization have been put in place correctly: Has the new team been set up? Is the new process working? Have the IT systems made the transition? Have we completed the necessary layoffs? Or the input measures can sometimes be more sophisticated: If we reorganized sales, have sales calls increased? If we changed our R&D process, are the stages toward commercialization being completed quicker? If we improved accountability in operations, is uptime increasing?

Both of these types of input measures are necessary, but they are not sufficient. Reminding ourselves that reorganization is a business issue like any other, let's take the analogy of a product launch. At the end of the product development, once the product has been launched, would we judge our success purely on whether the product was intrinsically a good idea and whether we met all our plans to launch it? Would we argue that the ultimate sales figures of the product had nothing to do with us and are other people's responsibility? Perhaps we would, but, if so, then our organization has much deeper problems! Ideally, we would not measure success from inputs only. We would judge the success of the product according to its sales. So too with reorgs. We should return to the business objectives we set for the project in step 1 and closely monitor these outputs to measure our success. Likewise, we should revisit the cost of the change, both the financial and the human cost and any lessons learned that the organization can apply in future changes. Of course, if, like so many reorganizations, we failed to set any business targets for the benefits or costs of the reorganization in the first place, we will never know whether it was successful or not.

This may come as bad news if you are midway through a reorganization and you have no clue what business outputs it is supposed to deliver. Our advice is this: although ascribing a business rationale to your reorg later in the process is not ideal, it is never too late. Try to force some kind of clarity on the business rationale for the reorg. Use some of the data given in chapter 1 to persuade your colleagues. That way, you will at least be able to judge whether you have been successful.

Pitfall 2: Letting Issues Fester

Reality never matches paper plans exactly. As Nancy McKinstry, the CEO of Wolters Kluwer, told us: "It is unrealistic to expect the new organization to work perfectly from the beginning. You have to live with and digest it, and rapidly course-correct when you find issues." This does not mean that you need to do a 180-degree flip-flop in the design as soon as you encounter a problem. Rather, the secret is to spot the teething problems of the new organization and fix them as soon as possible, in line with the logic of your original plans.

Unfortunately, many leaders hold firm to their paper plans, come what may. This becomes an even bigger problem when the reorganization was essentially incomplete: notably where it only covered lines and boxes and ignored people and process issues. The organization gets confused as it sees that the old processes no longer work, with multiple new interfaces and accountabilities unclear. If left unaddressed, these problems can last for years. For example, in one company that we know, which changed from a geographic-based organization to a product-based one, the local CEOs, who were left in place but shorn of their accountabilities and resources, mounted a guerrilla war against the new organization for several years after its launch, destroying the reorg's value. Lord Browne has this reminder for executives: "Your people are sometimes aware of what is going on before you are, so you need to listen to them. I do think that, especially with a radical reorganization, you need to understand what people's issues really are and report on them, not just tell people what you want. Two-way discussion is very important."

A better solution—that employed by Amelia and John above—is to be alive to the issues and react to fix them as soon as you spot them. Of course, this approach is by definition reactive. You may not know where to look. And you are reliant on people bringing the problems to the leadership when you need them to. Not all companies have this culture of openness. While you are trying to stop issues from festering, sometimes they still fester a little—and you risk losing some of the support for the reorg to cynicism, as we saw in the case of Amelia and John's company.

The best answer is to have a formal approach to identify the issues as proactively as possible. Of course, this means knowing where to look. As reorganization practitioners, we have seen enough reorgs to recognize a distinct patterns of problems. But from your position, as someone leading your own reorg, you can draw on the debates, worries, questions, and difficult decisions you have been involved with so far to identify the likely problems. Once you have done this, there are two formal mechanisms that really help. The first is setting *early warning metrics* to alert you to problems. So, for example, if you think that the sales force might be struggling with the new model, start viewing the numbers for different regions more often, and if you see dips right after the reorg, intervene to help the sales team resolve any issues (not to beat them up!). The second formal mechanism is a 5,000-mile check, where you bring in some of the original reorg team to stress-test the results. A good time to plan this is after one or two cycles of reporting management results so that you can look at business results as well as the morale and engagement of staff in the new organization and investigate underlying issues. In a fast-moving service business, this checkup could be after one month. In a slower, capital-intensive business, it could be after three.

Pitfall 3: Going Back to Business as Usual

Do you recognize the following description? We have all been working at the reorg for many months, maybe years. It has taken over our lives, and we want them back. We spend maybe 40 percent of our time working on the reorg, but our boss still expects us to perform our day jobs. We are tired, and our home lives are suffering. Several times we have snapped at colleagues or partners or children. We find it difficult to remember what the reorg was for in the first place. Our biggest wish: get it over and done with. What will we do then? *Go back to business as usual.* Our leaders (or we ourselves, if we are the leaders), sensing this mood, even make this a formal request of the business: the reorg is over; let's get back to business as usual, folks!

In many cases, this situation is exacerbated by launching a top-down reorganization (see step 3), which was not really necessary: a surgical, bottom-up reorg would have worked much better. The reorg team starts with the CEO and his or her reports and changes the first few layers of the organization. And because the process drags out so long, the reorg fizzles out at some point, way above the front line (the people who deliver the work and value). As pointed out earlier, the leaders of the reorg sometimes congratulate themselves by saying, "Look, we managed risk effectively by not changing the majority of people's jobs." (Note that we also failed to deliver any value, as we focused purely on a management merry-go-round.)

So, what was the reorg for? Well, if we also failed to set any business targets (step 1) and failed to measure the outputs of the reorg (see the previous pitfall), then your guess is as good as anyone's. The reorg is simply an albatross around our necks. Well, if you buy into the logic in this book so far, you will agree that this way of thinking—while understandable—is a symptom of failure. Given that reorgs are not fun from an entertainment perspective, *the only purpose of a reorg is to deliver business value* (cutting costs or delivering higher revenues). And it succeeds by changing the way people work. At scale. So, now is the time to tell the troops, "Let's start the new way of working—the one that is going to deliver all the reduced costs or higher revenues that we have all been talking about." Otherwise, why did we put ourselves and our colleagues through all this?

Pitfall 4: Forgetting the Whole Business

So, you have just been through a reorganization. Hopefully, following the lessons of this book, it delivered the value it was supposed to when it was supposed to. No doubt, there are some things that were challenging along the way. You and your colleagues learned something (perhaps you learned that you never wanted to do another reorg!). However, chances are your company will do a reorg again—perhaps not immediately and perhaps not in the same area, but in a different function or business unit. And as we have discussed in this book, most reorgs experience similar problems. So, would it not be helpful to try to capture the lessons of this reorganization in a somewhat formal way, to make sure that you (or your colleagues, if you do successfully dodge the next reorg) might learn from them, exactly as you might do for a capital project or product launch? Of course it would. But this practice happens seldom, or never—probably because everyone involved is too occupied recovering, putting the damn thing behind them, and returning to *business as usual* (the very phrase suggesting that nothing bad like this will happen again). However, as change in the business environment accelerates, we are seeing more and more reorgs.

So far, we have never come across a company that does capture the lessons of reorgs in a systematic way. This may seem like great news for reorganization consultants, but it is less good news for companies. In reality, it is also not very exciting for reorg consultants either: life is not fun if you solve the same basic problems over and over again. Reorganizations have problems enough, and it would be more interesting to us if companies learned how to solve the basic problems themselves and sought external advice on the more challenging issues. If your company does capture these lessons in a structured way, please get in touch with us and let us know how you do it.

In the absence of a formal approach to capture the lessons, the next best solution—which we have seen—is to maintain a record of the leaders and staff who have been involved in reorgs so that they can be called on to help in future ones. Often, these people are drawn from HR. As you will probably have seen, some of the skills you need to deliver all the steps of a reorganization—financial modeling, project management, meeting facilitation, conflict resolution—are not found in the standard HR tool kit. For this reason, the oil and gas company BP has gone beyond simply keeping a list of people involved in reorganizations and has developed a standard approach and training for its HR professionals to run reorgs (winning the 2015 Learning and Performance Institute Award for Social and Collaborative Learning for the IT platform it developed to do this).

. . .

As you read the pitfalls for this step, you will probably have realized that there are two causes of problems. The first, and easiest to fix, is that, having had a successful reorganization, you fail to go the final mile to maximize its value. The second challenge is more difficult to deal with. Having fallen into many of the pitfalls described in the previous chapters, you are now living through the inevitable negative consequences. We hope that you have read this book in time to have caught some of these traps at an earlier stage in your reorg.

For the final time, we will now share some cases of how to address these pitfalls.

Winning Way 1: Measure Both Outputs and Inputs

Let's return to the media case we first encountered in step 3. The company was moving from a very localized set of businesses to an organization focused on specific customer segments (business lines) so that the company could take advantage of its global scale. Clearly, a lot of detailing and planning happened after the initial work on the high-level concept (splitting into business lines) that we described earlier in this book. After that, the reorg team worked to detail how to make this split happen at the individual-country level (especially in Europe, where two business lines were very much intertwined).

As always, we found that life is more complicated in reality than in theory. In some countries, the clear distinction between these two customer segments did not exist; in others, pending M&As or lack of leadership, or both, caused challenges. But by focusing on transforming 80 percent of the business by revenues and profits and limiting exceptions to legitimate reasons, we navigated our way through. This was a case where our involvement was periodic. What really made the difference was a strong internal team that drove the reorg and ensured continuity from step to step.

This experience enabled us to set *input metrics* to measure the transition: the number of countries that had made the split and the closeness of the match between the accounting split of the two problematic customer segments and the organizational split. Obviously, real life meant that one business line would have to cross-sell for the other. But as the rationale behind the entire reorganization was revenue growth, the principle of the reorg was that a local business-line leader should be able to control 90 percent of his or her revenues.

Input metrics are nice to have, so that you can check whether you are doing what you planned to. But the outputs—in this case increased revenues in the new business lines—were more important. There was therefore an intense focus on the revenue growth that resulted from the new organization. At the same time, a note of realism had to come in here. The new European head for the segment with the greatest growth potential had to get up to speed in a very new job, start by sorting out the biggest markets, and then move on to the others. The reorganization did not fix everything overnight. However, within two years of the reorg, the company had moved from flatline growth to a healthy 5 percent annual growth rate. Looking back, the CEO now thinks that the reorg was "one of the smartest things I ever did. Without that new organization, we would not have been able to grow. The value of that growth far outweighed the disruption caused by the reorganization."

Winning Way 2: The 5,000-Mile Check

In a continuation of the case of the leading industrial-services company from the previous chapter, a month after launching the new organization, the executive in charge of the business unit called us back to complete a 5,000-mile check. As described earlier, the business unit had been split into two units in each geographical location: one focused on a high-tech, high-value, but declining business and the other a more operational, lower-margin, high-growth business. The people and processes were in place, and the first cycle of financial reporting was being completed.

The first thing we did was assess how accurately the revenues and costs had been mapped to the new organizational units. We knew that the two sub-business units (high-value versus low-cost) had very different profitability profiles, so we identified the locations where the P&L results diverged from our expectations. Happily, these divergences represented less than a 5 percent potential error in the P&L, suggesting that the reorg had been implemented with a high degree of accuracy. For the locations with the divergent results, we conducted further investigations into individual cost lines and work orders to understand how the costs and revenues were being allocated between the two sub-business units. In some of these cases, the apparent anomaly had a sound business rationale. In others, we found that the revenues and costs had indeed been misallocated. The most common reason turned out to be the copy-paste approach of previous work orders. With this knowledge, we were able to provide additional, detailed guidance to local financial controllers to ensure that the second month of financial reporting would be even more accurate.

Second, we conducted a survey of staff, polling a wide cross-section of the organization—including all the different geographical locations and levels of the organization. The survey asked respondents to rate the benefits and challenges of the reorg and the help provided by the central team. Responses were anonymous, but the demographic information enabled us to identify particular locations or levels in the organization where embedding the new way of working was proving more challenging. We also asked respondents to provide examples where the new organization was already adding impact, either in terms of increased sales or in opportunities for efficiency. These stories proved useful in identifying opportunities that could be rolled out elsewhere in the organization and in providing marketing material to promote the new organization through internal communications.

Finally, we created a detailed plan to help the business unit's leadership to deliver the increased revenues and efficiencies that were expected of the new organization. This plan focused especially on the growing, operational sub-business unit, where most of the changes were focused. Working with the new leader of this sub-business unit and his team, we defined around forty-five actions, grouping them into seven categories, and identified business outcomes for each category. We created a plan with milestones that enabled the executive in charge of the business unit and her team to performance-manage the transformation.

Winning Way 3: Change the Way of Working

As we have tried to emphasize throughout the book, changing structures (reporting lines, roles, governance, etc.) alone is not enough. Successful reorganizations change people, process, and structure (numbers, capabilities, mind-sets, and behavior) together, and those changes reinforce each other.

For example, a worldwide logistics company that we worked with decided that it needed to start behaving more globally to better serve global clients that wanted joined-up services across geographic areas. They moved some of the accountabilities, particularly those for developing complex supply-chain products suitable for more sophisticated global clients and relationship management with global clients, to the center. This arrangement was not straightforward as the country-based business units continued to deliver these services.

The company discovered that after the structure changed and, indeed, after the processes were adjusted (so that the global units had decision rights in relation to global clients), most people did not change their behavior. We therefore diagnosed the existing culture using a culture survey. It showed that the company had a strong operational culture but was still relatively weak at collaboration, innovation, and awareness of its competitors and customers. To address those weaknesses, the company's leaders decided that increased collaboration was needed across the entire organization and that innovation and external awareness were critical in the global units focusing on global clients.

The company then created a set of interventions to move staff mind-sets and behaviors. These covered four elements:

- **Clear communication about why collaboration was important:** this message involved storytelling (which is always more powerful than merely listing facts) and a variety of other forms of communication (not just e-mail).

- **Changes to incentives:** the most critical action was to change metrics so that both the countries and the global units were rewarded for capturing and then serving the new customers.

- **Capability building:** this activity was mainly done in small groups, in country, where teams talked through how best to collaborate.

- **Role modeling:** this tactic started very deliberately with the senior team, for the first time ever, as they collaborated visibly on global projects.

Making these cultural changes alongside the structural and process changes was hard work and required substantial time from the leadership team. It also took a while for the organization to change (leaders started to report increases in collaboration after six months, but it was almost two years before the changes became fully embedded). However, when these changes did happen, it altered what people were doing day to day within the new organizational structure. Changing structure alone is like changing your car. Changing processes and people is like changing how you drive that car to take advantage of all its new features.

Winning Way 4: Capture the Lessons

As mentioned above, we have not yet seen a company that captures the lessons of a reorg to the degree that is really required. If your company is the exception, please let us know how you do it. We encourage you to share your experiences of past reorgs and current ones at the book's website, www.reorg.book.com. In any case, we hope that businesses may take note and themselves develop ways of recording the lessons learned.

For now, we will attempt to sketch out what this way of capturing lessons could look like in the final installment of our utility company case.

After a week of late nights, finalizing a number of difficult, last-minute management moves and ensuring that everything was in place for the reorganization, Amelia is again clearing her desk to return to her day job—for now. Before finishing, she put two things in place. First, with John and the management team, she designed a scorecard of metrics to measure the reorganization's success. As much as possible, she has tried to use metrics already in existence to minimize the burden on the business, but has measured them more often and has passed the metrics on to a more senior level in the organization—to the CEO (John) and his chief of staff. These metrics cover several areas:

- The outputs expected from the reorganization: lower-cost capital projects, lower people costs, and higher trading revenues

- The inputs of the reorganization, such as the percentage of people in new roles, the layoff letters issued, and the training sessions run for those moving into new jobs

- The cost of the change, including the financial costs incurred (e.g., the cost of any third-party support or outplacement services) and the human cost (i.e., the number of people affected and the impact on employee engagement and retention)

In light of the months of debate around the reorg, Amelia has also highlighted the metrics that apply to risk. In particular, the metrics to be measured include the schedule performance for capital projects versus plan, where confusion about the new process could lead to slower times; the availability of the plant, especially in countries that have had large people reductions; the schedule for projects; decreases in staff morale during the change; and the accuracy of the P&L split between trading and generation (given that some assumptions were being made around transfer prices).

The second thing that Amelia has put in place is a plan for a formal 5,000-mile check of the reorganization two months after D-day. Through John, she has already secured agreement for some key members of her team to rejoin her for a three-week period to conduct this review. As mentioned earlier, each member of her reorganization team has found a rewarding position in the new organization.

With these plans in place, Amelia is able to enjoy the period after D-day. The reorganization is a success, the naysayers are proved wrong, and indeed some of the naysayers who were unable to adapt to the new approaches have been asked to exit the business (though the majority have adapted and some have become supporters).

In the first week of the new organization, John again holds two webcasts (which he and Amelia prepared together) for the entire firm. He thanks all the members of the organization for their patience and support through a difficult time: a number of valued colleagues have exited the business, and others have had to move with their families to new locations—often new countries. He reminds them why the company made these moves: first, to cut costs to be able to survive but, second, to develop capabilities that will enable the firm to win against its competitors. He reminds them that the reorganization is only the beginning: it is like a football team (or, he tells the American staff, a soccer team) deciding which formation it wants to use, selecting the right players, and coming up with the plan for the match. Now it is up to the team to play in a different way and to win that match. Using the work that the reorg team had done earlier on people and processes, John reminds his staff that many of them will need to work in a very different way—in particular, in capital projects, operations, and trading. He tells them that these are the qualities by which future leaders of the company will be selected. Of course, some people are yet to be convinced. But John keeps hammering home this message in all his speeches, visits, and management meetings and pushes his leadership team to do the same.

Two months later . . . Amelia is enjoying her position as a senior member of the new central capital projects function. Using her knowledge of frontline work and connections across the organization, she is making sure the new governance process the team is putting in place is practical and nonbureaucratic and reflects the needs of the market units. She has received a few calls from the CEO's chief of staff, who has let her know the action that he has taken when the reorg metrics revealed teething problems with the new organization. Now it is time to run the 5,000-mile checkup.

Amelia's team reviews the results of the last two cycles of P&L reporting for power generation and trading, comparing results across countries. Where some countries' proportions are wildly different, the team members conduct interviews to understand how the transfer price and allocation process has worked. In most cases, they find a logical explanation: in others, rules need to be adapted or reinforced.

The team also issues an online survey across a cross-section of affected people in the organization, asking them to evaluate the changes, highlight issues, and provide suggestions. The survey is kept anonymous from management, but Amelia and her team can see where the biggest problems have been, by grade and location. They are then able to follow up through interviews with the leaders. The main issue usually turns out to be insufficient communication of the changes. Despite their efforts, some people assumed that the reorg would be "just another of those changes" and did not pay full attention. With the organization now largely working well, Amelia initiates another round of communication efforts to clarify the main questions. In one area, her own—capital projects—a significant change is required. The reorg team had envisaged a centralized team of *engineering technical authorities* to sign off on any variation to standards. It seems that this centralization of authority has been a step too far, slowing down work, so Amelia recommends reverting to the old system of local technical authorities, while retaining the other central functions.

Having identified the final tweaks required for the new organization, Amelia holds a formal lessons-learned session with John and her team. The group walks through the five stages of the reorg process and identifies the pitfalls the effort fell into and the most successful actions the team took. Using the information from this meeting, Amelia captures the main actions from the reorg, the recommendations for dealing with the pitfalls better next time around, and the successes that future reorg leaders should remember. Amelia's report is then made available to the head of HR and business and function heads, together with members of HR worldwide, who are encouraged to refer to it for future reorgs.

Amelia returns to her thoughts at the beginning of the reorg. The signs so far are that she has delivered a successful reorganization: cost has been reduced, and there are some early signs of opportunities captured through the centralized trading function. Of course, the proof of the pudding will be seen when the new organization delivers its business targets. As a reward, her own career has been accelerated. She now has a more senior role and relishes her new challenges. And her concerns? There have been difficult conversations, no doubt. But she has not alienated her bosses, her colleagues, or the workforce. Even when they have disagreed with her, leaders and staff have seemed to appreciate her commitment to following the right way of doing things. It has certainly been a different experience from the other reorgs she has seen. "Maybe I would not mind running another reorg, sometime in the future," she muses.

—THE END

Managing Communications in Step 5

- **Staff and leadership needs:** Now that the new organization is running, you might mistakenly feel that people's need to understand it has been met. But remember, it is not the change described in the PowerPoint documents that matters; it is real people doing their jobs differently. So far, leaders and staff have been engaged with the new organization at an intellectual level. Now they need to understand it at a practical level: how do they do their jobs differently? This new understanding will lead to different questions—including ones that you have never considered before. With the best motivation in the world, your paper plans will not work out perfectly in reality. Some things will not work as well as planned, leaders and staff will notice, and they will expect redress.

- **What to communicate:** In this step, you need to go back to the business objectives of the reorg: the one big idea of the reorg and the three to five major organizational changes to deliver on that big idea. The reorg is just one step in delivering these business results. As Iain Conn, the CEO of Centrica and former CEO of BP's downstream business, told us: "You need to spend eighteen months to two years saying the same thing. Because if people hear the CEO repeating the same things over and over again, they see that it remains important and it becomes embedded in day-to-day priorities." In addition, communication back from the front line becomes much more important. Rather than claim that everything is perfect (it never is), you should open your ears to the feedback from the business to understand the teething issues of the new organization and the suggestions for how to address them. Of course, these should be discriminating ears: some complaints will be from those who dislike change. But others will be invaluable in helping you make course corrections and deliver the business results that you need.

- **How to communicate:** Because the most important communication in this step is bottom-up, you should retain the mechanism for two-way communications (e.g., reorg e-mail) but also make it clear to your leaders that you expect them to regularly check how the new organization is working and to communicate issues upward on a fixed timetable (e.g., every month). It can also be useful to put in place specific mechanisms for tracking how things are going: for example, a transition monitoring team.[1]

Step 5 Summary

Pitfalls	Winning Ways
• Only measuring inputs	• Measure both outputs and inputs
• Letting issues fester	• Conduct a 5,000-mile check
• Going back to business as usual	• Change the way of working
• Forgetting the whole business	• Capture the lessons

How to Use These Ideas in Your Organization

- Remember that this is the step where many of the pitfalls of the previous steps manifest themselves. Try to address these earlier in the process.

- In reality, paper plans never work out exactly the way you intend. Do not think your reorg will be perfect (it never is), and be prepared to make course corrections.

- Use a mixture of metrics, surveys, and interviews to proactively uncover issues for resolution.

- Plan for your reorg project team to return to conduct a 5,000-mile check (using a list of questions such as those in the template in appendix D), one or two management reporting cycles after implementation (so they can also review the accuracy of the business results and the reorg's impact on them). In some cases this can be done through a simple "pulse survey" of employees to test the effectiveness of the change.

- Do not declare victory for your reorg until it delivers the business results you wanted (this will be some time after the actual implementation).

- Capture your own lessons learned. Create a companywide repository of these lessons—a repository leaders and HR have access to, and if you wish, share them with us to help improve business knowledge of the issues.

8

Bringing It All Together

f you have read through the whole book, many thanks for your attention. We hope that you now feel more confident about the success of your reorganization. If you have jumped to this chapter from the start, then welcome and we hope you will dip into some of the preceding chapters to get more of the detail.

We are not going to try to repeat every point from the book here. But we do want to reiterate the two most important messages we urge you to take away. First, a reorg is like any other business problem: you need to understand the benefits the reorganization may bring, the costs and risks you face, and the time and effort it will take to deliver.

Second, you are reorganizing people, and what you do affects their careers, incomes, job satisfaction, and well-being. As Rob Rosenberg, HR director of DHL Supply Chain, told us: "I am constantly reminded about how important it is for the leader to walk the talk, and, when leading the reorganization, how microscopically you are viewed and the importance of verbal and nonverbal cues. You need to maintain an open mind to understand people's problems. If we were to do this over again, we would have done more up front to acknowledge what individuals are going through personally." John Ferraro, the former COO of EY, echoes this: "Command and control increasingly does not work. You have to be inclusive in how you run things and how you reorganize. Leaders need empathy, humility, and a sense of purpose that everyone can rally around."

So, in addition to delivering the business results, you need to design your approach to be as caring as possible to all your employees—both those who stay and those who leave. At the heart of this is the engagement that we talked about at the start. It is critical to communicate through this process because most employees hate these kind of changes, but they hate secrecy and uncertainty more. Even if all you can communicate is timelines, it is better to do that than not to communicate. Above all, don't underestimate how distressing a reorganization can be, and for this reason, try to get it completed as quickly as you can so that people can move on and start making the new organization work. Fortunately, this is also the right outcome from a business point of view: by acting quickly, you will minimize the costs and risks and deliver the benefits sooner.

In this book, we have described five steps to go through during the process of the reorganization, together with the pitfalls and success factors (table 8-1). These steps are all critical: it is never right to skip a step, although in smaller, simpler reorganizations, you may be able to complete a step relatively quickly.

Both the pitfalls and the winning ways are based on our direct experience of leading over twenty-five major reorganizations and our involvement in many hundreds more. So, even if you think you would never fall into one of these pitfalls, do keep an eye out for them, as we know many very smart and capable executives who have run into these snags.

Reorganization is not easy. In fact, a common issue is that it is perceived as easier than it actually is: redrawing lines and boxes is simple, but implementing all the things we have discussed in this book is not. On the one hand, it is the difference between drawing a cartoon and designing a detailed engineering blueprint; on the other, it is the difference between sitting in a room with friendly collaborators to come up with a plan, and presenting a controversial plan to the organization. But we are confident that if you follow these steps and bear in mind the lessons from others

TABLE 8-1

Summary of the five-step process for reorganizations

Step	Pitfalls	Winning ways
1. Construct the reorg's profit and loss	• Benefits ill defined • No consideration of resources required • No agreed-on timeline	• Explicitly define value • Identify costs and risks • Set an accelerated timeline
2. Understand current weaknesses and strengths	• Focusing only on weaknesses • Only listening to leaders • Relying on hearsay	• Identify strengths to preserve • Make sure you hear everyone's views • Triangulate with analysis
3. Choose from multiple options	• Skipping steps 1 and 2 • Focusing only on lines and boxes • Imposing one generic solution • Going around difficult leaders	• Don't skip steps 1 and 2! • Cover people, process, and structure • Explore different options • Have the leadership debate now
4. Get the plumbing and wiring right	• Long, sequential planning and evolutionary implementation • Leaving leaders in old positions to resist change • Trying to change everything, or changing nothing • Confusing your people	• Plan in parallel, implement as a revolution • Give leaders a stake in the new organization • Identify the 80% to change, do that in 100% detail • Create the cookbook
5. Launch, learn, and course-correct	• Only measuring inputs • Letting issues fester • Going back to business as usual • Forgetting the lessons	• Measure both outputs and inputs • Conduct a 5,000-mile check • Change the way of working • Capture the lessons

who have successfully—and sometimes not so successfully—followed this path before, you will create a new organization that will both deliver the business value you were expecting and take into account the human needs of your staff.

Cost-Driven Reorgs

t is, unfortunately, often the case that at least one reason for a reorganization is to reduce costs.[1] Our advice here would always be to stop and consider if there are alternatives before reducing head count, because in addition to the human cost, there are significant reputational as well as disruption costs. We have seen many organizations reduce costs without significant head-count reduction through various other means:

- Reducing non-head-count spending (travel, training, accommodation, legal costs, consulting costs, and so on). We would always advise looking at the full set of indirect costs of the organization before deciding how much cost needs to come out of personnel alone.

- Redeployment of head count to growth areas if the skills of the staff being moved are appropriate for the new roles.

- Offering leaves of absence instead of layoffs during periods of lower demand.

If none of these is possible, you need to start looking at the actions below, but when implementing them, you should try doing so through natural attrition as people move out of the organization. This approach is less disruptive and will reduce layoff costs but, of course, means that the savings will take longer to be realized. Nevertheless, if significant personnel reductions are likely, all of the advice from earlier in the book is especially relevant: be transparent on the process, and move as quickly as possible to minimize the upset for people involved.

We would also advise against making cost reduction the only aim of a reorganization (although, by the same token, it should never be concealed if it is part of the motivation). Reorganizations are an opportunity to reorient an organization to make it operate more effectively. As people are being disrupted anyway, it is an opportunity to consider revenue benefits as well as costs. Even in the most challenging cost turnaround, it is important to have some chink of light around revenues. Companies that only cut costs often go out of business. As Neil Hayward, group people director of the UK Post Office, told us: "Our big learning is that efficiency—in our case, cutting functions within our organiza-tion's silos—is easy to achieve but only scratches the surface and will not be long-term sustainable. You only get real gains on long-term effectiveness. But this is harder to get to."

Taking costs out of an organization is not easy. Here's an example of how things can go wrong. An international energy company that needed to save money fast started by simply defining the amount of savings it needed and then required each department to cut costs by a similar amount, primarily through head-count reductions, which varied from 17 to 22 percent. The reality, however, was that the company needed to invest more in certain technological areas that were changing quickly, as well as in operations, where performance was far below industry benchmarks. What's more, the HR and IT departments substantially duplicated certain activities because dif-ferent layers in the organization were doing similar things. Much deeper cuts should therefore have been made in these functions, with little strategic risk. But the company cut costs across the board, and just six months later, technology and operations were lobbying hard to bring in new staff to take on an "uncontrollable workload," while substantial duplication remained in HR and IT.

We suggest that a better way would be to start by understanding your business strategy and, within the strategy, which activities drive value and which activities do or could make the organization competitively distinctive. In the public and nonprofit sectors, good proxies for these activities might be delivery of policy outcomes, number of people helped out of poverty, events staged, school performances, etc. When you have done this, then you need to invest in the value-creating activities and cut the costs in others.

The changes that result from this kind of thinking can be dramatic. A government-funded environmental organization, for example, spent a lot of time on monitoring individual species and campaigning against their extinction rather than on climate change, which the organization's leaders actually regarded as more important and where they could have a greater impact. The organization took cost-cutting as an opportunity to look intensely at what it did. It decided to stop the extinction-related lobbying and policy activities, undertaken by about 20 percent of its employees, and instead move the work of another 20 percent of its staff— along with some of the people who had been undertaking the extinction work—into other nonprofits with suitable mandates. The organization then reinvested a large portion of the savings to increase the number of staff members working on climate change. It also invested in building the capabilities of its relatively weak HR and finance functions. The result was an organization that was significantly smaller and lower cost but also one that had been strengthened in delivering its most important purpose. It also meant that the organization's story, although difficult, was not just about cost-cutting but was also about how the group was going to be able to make a real difference in critical areas of public policy.

Getting to practicalities, eight savings ideas can help to identify pure cost savings and put objective facts behind decisions that can be emotional and contentious. As you will see, all these ideas, apart from the first one, involve a detailed understanding of the *activities* undertaken in an organization, not only its head count.

1. **Change spans and layers.** Leaders are used to seeing their organizations represented as boxes and lines. Try instead to show your organization (whether the full company or a part of it) as a demographic pyramid of the numbers of people at different levels. To the side, note the average *span of control* (manager to direct report) ratio. The results may surprise you: the chart may not look like a pyramid at all. In many cases, you will see a burgeoning middle layer with limited spans of control. In others, there can be a whole layer whose role is questionable and which could be removed. Significant savings can be achieved by working out how to maximize spans of control to appropriate proportions or removing a whole layer of the organization, making sure to reinvest some of the savings in improving the quality and, sometimes, the quantity of the management layer(s) that remains.

2. **Transfer activities.** Without laying off any employees, you can sometimes in-source activities that have, until now, been done by contractors. For example, with a utility we worked with, we found that an area of the operations workforce was heavily unionized. But the union was happy to work with us to understand which activities could be transferred in from contractors and carried out by company technicians. It was also happy to agree to work on performance improvements together and commit to higher outputs as part of this agreement.

3. **Lean out activities.** This is the typical savings approach of *operational improvements*, rather than *organizational changes*, and the process improvements from reorganizations often focus more on clarity of roles and effectiveness than on savings. Nevertheless, it is sometimes possible

to run a traditional operations improvement program (identifying savings ideas, piloting them, and then scaling up) in tandem with a reorganization and use the reorg to embed operational changes in the organization. We have experienced doing this through a field force transformation where the lessons from operational changes in the field and the ideas on organizational changes in HQ came together in a common set of proposals. Some changes focused on cost, and others focused on effectiveness: for example, creating a new role that literally led to 90 percent savings in one area of work, through more-effective contractor management.

4. **Remove activities.** Often, when a leader has an idea and launches a project, a team is set up to deliver it. Very infrequently will this team declare victory, pack its bags, and go back to other activities. The team stays and the activity becomes—our favorite phrase again—*business as usual.* Alternatively, activities that were critical in the past become redundant because of changes in the business. Rather than simply cutting head count and expecting workers to deliver the same outcomes by working harder or cutting corners, leaders need to identify these discretionary or low-value activities and stop them.

5. **Reduce the frequency of activities.** Another way of reducing costs is to conduct some activities less frequently, for example, internal audits, benchmarking of pay, and internal management reporting. Of course, these decisions need to be weighed against the value at risk, but the decisions do not always point in just one direction (i.e., doing more). In the oil and gas industry, for example, compressors are typically maintained (taken apart and checked) every year. It turns out that this schedule can

lead to the equipment's breaking more often. Leaving the compressor alone and instead monitoring its condition can often save money *and* improve performance.

6. **Centralize activities.** In many companies, the same activities are replicated many times across the organization. Typically, support services—such as HR, finance, IT, corporate affairs, and communications—fall into this category. Other examples include strategy and major projects (above a certain cost), whereas sales and operations typically need to be located locally. Here we need to draw the distinction between centralization of activities in one or more geographical places and centralization of reporting lines. Only the former leads to real cost savings (through the capacity to cover each other's work, run similar tasks together, prioritize better, etc.). For the latter, it is important to have one person able to understand and make decisions on a whole function, but centralizing reporting lines does not deliver savings by itself (except in spans and layers). Centralizing the right activities can lead to improved effectiveness as well as efficiencies (e.g., developing one standard, more efficient way of doing things). But be careful: some things are better done locally. Take HR as an example: compensation and benefits, payroll, recruitment, and training are mainly transactional activities that can be centralized. However, HR advice on business issues (usually called *business partners*) always needs to be close to the manager who needs it—that is, local.

7. **Move activities.** In a global market, high skills and good language abilities (especially English) are available in lower-cost countries around the world. The movement of activities is a constantly evolving picture: in 2016, Chinese

companies were also seeing activities shift from mainland China to other, cheaper areas in East Asia. Typically, the activities to consider for this savings approach are the same transactional activities as for centralizing activities (you simply centralize them in lower-cost areas). For global companies, twenty-four-hour access can obviously also be a factor and normally leads to a selection of three or four lower-cost countries across the world. Critical to the success of these moves is knowledge of how to establish yourself in these countries, so either colocation with operations or advice from a company with experience in this area is essential. Of course, the cost of the latter needs to be priced into any savings case.

8. **Automate activities.** As with people who talk to you about bizarre organizational concepts, when people start bamboozling you with obscure IT words and stories about how it all worked out so well in similar companies, it is time to run for the hills! Automation can, of course, lead to huge savings. However, the savings will only happen with activities that you understand and can control. With one company we know, automation led to a savings of 20 to 30 percent for activities that were already under control. For those that were not understood, costs increased as much as sevenfold in some cases. Unless there is a common IT system already in place, we would advise running a new process first, even with IT workarounds, to make sure that it runs as effectively as possible, before applying an IT solution. Be very careful to understand what the system you are choosing covers and what it does not (or you will find out that it costs you more when you have to add in an additional, essential element of the system later). And try to

understand what flexibility your IT system brings: ossifying your processes in a very inflexible system that fails to communicate with other systems is obviously a bad idea in an age of IT innovation.

Using a very structured approach to identify savings across the organization and basing everything on facts about activities will help you navigate your way through a topic that can quickly become emotional and upsetting. If the decision means that headcount reductions are required, you owe it to your colleagues to follow the most rigorous and fair way of delivering those savings, rather than succumbing to the horse trading that can so often result. In describing how the UK Post Office cut head count by 12 percent, yet increased staff satisfaction, Neil Hayward pointed out three factors: "Firstly, a coordinated, joined-up program of the cuts rather than a piecemeal approach. Secondly, face-to-face discussions and engagement with people on the change. And thirdly, creating a good working relationship with the unions so that they understood it, even if they did not like it."

Appendix B

M&A-Driven Reorgs

One very specific flavor of reorg is that conducted through an M&A. As noted in the introduction, merger-driven reorgs seem to experience particular problems. Only 8 percent of merger reorgs fully deliver their objectives in the planned time, and 41 percent—way more than other types of reorgs—take longer than expected. And in 10 percent of cases, the reorg brought about by the merger actually harms the organization. Unpacking the reasons why and providing definitive guidance probably requires an additional book. Below we provide some pointers to more successful outcomes based on the five-step process.

While the five steps still apply, the way they play out can be quite different. On the upside of an M&A event, everyone knows that this is the biggest thing affecting the company, so you will be able to get the resources you need. On the downside, part of the equation (the challenges within the other company) remains opaque to you until quite late in the process. In addition, you have to be extremely careful about the information that is shared, given competition law. We find it very helpful to make explicit a small number—say, around seven—of memorable information-sharing rules to help navigate these sorts of issues. For example, a leader who will be the future head of a new business unit will obviously want to see the P&Ls of the units from the two companies that will come together under his or her leadership. Yet—depending on the competition law in the jurisdiction in question—this might not be allowed. For this reason, in merger situations, we start every presentation (our first PowerPoint slide) with a review of the competition rules to be compliant.

In this appendix, we lay out step by step the main differences to keep in mind when you are delivering an M&A-focused reorg.

Step 1: Construct the Reorg's Profit and Loss

- In many ways, the focus on P&L is front and center in an M&A: everyone is focused on the combined P&L of the new entity and has an interest in synergies and their rationale. In many cases, the synergies will be cost savings, and the advice in the previous appendix will again be relevant. The challenge is to understand the organizational implications of these synergy ideas.

Step 2: Understand the Current Weaknesses and Strengths

- For your own company, this step is clearly the same as for a traditional reorg. For the other company (acquired or merged), it may be more difficult to get a sense of the strengths and weaknesses before the deal is closed. However, you can get some insights from due-diligence enquiries, former members of the company (including those in your own organization), or the internet— whether through the company's own publications or sites such as LinkedIn, which enable you to profile individual managers. How you go about this step is also dependent on whether this is a takeover (where the default position is that the acquired organization will largely be absorbed into your company) or a true merger, where you may be looking for a best-of-breed approach from across the two companies, in terms of both the organization and its personnel.

Step 3: Choose from Multiple Options

- Before the deal closes, it is possible to develop a strong hypothesis for what the new organization will look like. In M&A situations, there is typically a lot of focus on the organizational structure (by definition, you will have to choose one structure that integrates the two companies and comes from one company or the other or is some combination of both). There is also usually a focus on people: both the numbers needed (as some of the synergies will clearly come from staff efficiencies) and a shared culture that needs to be created in the new company. However, it is important not to forget processes: companies normally go about their processes (whether they are deciding on strategy, launching a product or process, or running day-to-day operations) in very different ways, and confusion between these processes postmerger is a frequent problem. In addition, if this is the first of a series of M&As, you might also want to reconsider your current organizational setup to facilitate bolting on or integrating new organizational units.

Step 4: Get the Plumbing and Wiring Right

- Some planning and even quite detailed designs are possible before the deal closes. However, when the deal does close, partway through this step, you must quickly circle back on the hypotheses from previous steps—the assumptions on synergies (step 1), the understanding of the acquired company's strengths and weaknesses (step 2), and the concept design (step 3)—to confirm that they are sound and, where necessary, refine them. Then planning for the actual implementation can proceed apace. With M&As,

there is a typically a team dedicated to each area of the business, run by business professionals rather than HR—meaning that necessary resources are in place to deliver the reorg. In this step, communications to the wider workforce and to leaders worried about their positions is even more important than usual.

Step 5: Launch, Learn, and Course-Correct

- All the advice on step 5 in chapter 7 applies to an M&A, only more so. You need to measure business outputs against the original synergy plan. With many more assumptions about how the combined company will work, a formal 5,000-mile check is essential. With two cultures to bring together and different approaches to processes, there is an increased need to change the way of working. And if you plan to do more M&As, capturing the results of your experience for next time is critical.

The Legal Context of Reorgs in the European Union

Appendix C

I n every multinational reorganization we have undertaken, we encounter at some point the challenge of different legal frameworks for staff consultation in each country. Invariably, this challenge focuses on the legal framework of the European Union, which contrasts with other regions of the world (North America, Asia, the Middle East, etc.) where legal requirements are looser. Often, this means that the overall reorganization timeline is slowed down. Alternatively, business units outside the EU are forced to make greater changes (e.g., cut more costs) than those in Europe.

It does not need to be that way: proper planning can prevent subsequent slippages. Following winning way number 3 of step 4, you may have 80 percent of the organization follow one timeline and have the remainder follow a slower timeline. And by incorporating a period of real consultation (including a period for business units outside the EU), you may land on a better answer that ultimately delivers more quickly. Interestingly, the McKinsey surveys found that staff in Europe are less likely to disrupt a reorg than anywhere else in the world, with the exception of India. Clearly, a good process, followed well, can deliver the effective staff consultation you need.

This appendix provides an overview of the consultation obligations that apply to companies reorganizing within the EU. It does not purport to be a definitive statement of the law, not least because the laws of the member states of the EU are dynamic, as new precedents are developed, particularly through case law of the Court of Justice of the European Union (CJEU).

Any company planning a reorganization in the EU should seek specialist legal advice on its obligations as early as possible in the process—in step 1, when you define the reorg timeline.

General Principles

Many of the obligations that apply to reorgs in the EU derive from overarching framework directives. Unfortunately, though, it is not simply a case of reading the EU directive to understand the obligations that apply in every EU country. Because each member state of the EU has a fairly wide margin of discretion as to how the particular directive is implemented, there is no substitute for knowing the specific rules that apply in each member state.

The general principle is that in most cases the obligation to consult the workforce is an obligation to consult representatives of the workforce, rather than each member of the workforce individually (though there is sometimes an obligation of individual consultation, too). In most of the EU, this means consulting trade unions or work councils, whether the consultation is at a national, regional, or workplace level. For example, in the UK (at the time of this writing still part of the EU), a workforce representative body may sometimes be set up ad hoc to deal with particular issues, such as a business sale or large-scale layoffs.[1] This will require additional time to deal with the election of employee representatives before consultation can begin. For example, Hannah Meadley-Roberts at the European Bank of Reconstruction and Development told us: "We don't have anything that resembles a union. So we have a staff council. We found that we needed a voice for the staff when making changes. Having a group of people to speak on behalf of their peers to can make a really big difference."

It is important to check whether collective agreements with trade unions apply to the reorg in question. Such collective agreements, which can exist on a company, industrywide, or national level, can add additional obligations above and beyond the minimum legal obligations. Furthermore, in some countries, there is an obligation to negotiate a "social plan" to minimize the number of dismissals and their effect.

In this appendix, we focus mainly on the obligation to consult when there are multiple layoffs, but information and consultation obligations can arise in a wide variety of other circumstances in EU countries, including the sale of a business or part of a business, under the Acquired Rights Directive (Directive 2001/23/EC). Moreover, some cases carry an obligation to inform a relevant public authority—and not just the workforce—about the proposals.

For consultation to be effective in the EU, it needs to be *meaningful*. EU law normally expects that the consultation will begin early enough to allow the employee representatives to influence the nature and effect of the reorg and at the very least to ameliorate its consequences on displaced employees. However, in the majority of reorgs in most EU countries, the trade unions or works councils do not have veto power over your proposals.

Consultation for "Collective Redundancies"

When a company is contemplating making multiple "redundancies" (layoffs), it must consult with employee representatives in "good time" and "with a view to reaching agreement" in relation to those redundancies. This obligation arises from the Collective Redundancies Directive (Directive 98/59/EC).

Each member state of the EU is required to enact the principles of this directive into its own national law. For example, in the UK, as of 2016, the principles of this directive are enshrined in section 188 of the Trade Union and Labour Relations (Consolidation) Act 1992. This act provides that collective consultation must take place for a minimum of thirty days where the company proposes to dismiss as redundant (i.e., to lay off) twenty or more employees at one establishment within a period of ninety days, and for a minimum of forty-five days where it is proposed that one hundred or more employees may be redundant.

The level of certainty that is required for redundancies to be "contemplated" varies in each country according to the case law of that country. This could be quite early on in the reorg process. Ideally, the first communication of the reorg needs to be framed in terms that the company has not committed itself to proceeding with either the restructuring or the redundancies, so that employee consultation can still influence the company's decision. Remember that the e-mails and other documents you generate at an early stage when discussing the proposals internally might need to disclosed to a court in later legal proceedings in the event of a dispute over when consultation should have begun.

Consultation typically begins by giving information to employee representatives. The minimum written information that must be provided includes the following:

- The reasons for the proposed redundancies

- The number and categories of employees to be made redundant

- The number and categories of employees usually working at the company

- The period for implementing the proposed dismissals

- The proposed selection criteria

- The method for calculating redundancy payments

There are no hard and fast rules on how consultation should be conducted, but the company should be seen to take account of employee representatives' comments and respond to these comments, even if no agreement is ultimately reached. However, collective consultation must cover ways to accomplish the following measures:

- Avoiding redundancies or reducing the number of employees affected

- Mitigating the consequences of redundancies through social measures, such as redeployment or retraining

The obligation to consult operates, in effect, as a moratorium on the proposed dismissals, so that the dismissals cannot take effect for a minimum period (usually at least thirty days) once consultation has started and, if necessary, once the relevant public authority has been notified of the proposals.

There has been case law in relation to large-scale redundancies as to whether the company has to consult over the actual business decision to reorganize. The view has traditionally been that consultation over the business reasons for the reorg is not required. But whenever the reorg involves the closure of a business unit or site, it may be difficult to consult meaningfully without looking at the rationale for the reorganization in the first place. In the UK, there is case law that consultation over the business reasons for the reorg may be required in these circumstances.

Differences Between EU Member States

The exact period of consultation required is not prescribed by the directive and varies across member states. In France, for example, for companies employing more than fifty employees, the works council has to hold at least two meetings separated by a minimum of fifteen days and then has to give its opinion within two to four months, depending on the number of proposed dismissals. If the works council fails to deliver its opinion before the deadline, the council is deemed to have been properly consulted. When necessary, the works council may call in an outside expert of its choice, at the employer's expense, to advise the council on collective redundancies involving ten or more employees.

In Germany, the company must notify the employment agency, which is a state authority with local branches, of the proposed layoffs in writing before serving dismissal letters where mass layoffs are proposed, as follows:

- More than 5 employees in an establishment of 20 to 60 employees; or

- Ten percent or more than 25 employees in an establishment of 60 to 500 employees; or

- At least 30 employees in an establishment of 500 or more employees.

The employment will not end before expiry of the waiting period after notification (usually at least one month). Where the employees of the establishment have elected a works council and the layoffs are part of a wider operational reorganization, the company must, before serving notice of termination, engage in negotiations with the works council to reach a *reconciliation of interests* (Interessenausgleich).

These examples are used merely to give a flavor of the diverse requirements across just a handful of EU countries. Each country is different, and one size of consultation will not fit all.

Conclusion

If reorgs are to be addressed as a business problem, then collective consultation requirements should be too, although they may, hopefully, also form part of the solution. A well-planned and properly run consultation process can allow the company to engage its workforce in a relatively efficient and structured manner and may even result in agreement (although individual buy-in is a different matter). At the very least, the idea of consulting with trade unions for a month ought to focus business leaders at an early stage (somewhere between steps 1 and 3 of the process described in this book) on exactly what consequences for employees will follow from the planned reorg. European HR should be involved as early as possible in the planning stage to ensure that there are no nasty surprises.

In our experience, in a badly planned reorg, a state of panic can sometimes occur at a late stage, when a European HR specialist or lawyer informs the CEO that the project timetable is incompatible with the relevant consultation requirements in the EU countries concerned. For global organizations, this discrepancy in timing can often make the workforce in countries with more-liberal labor markets bear a disproportionate and unplanned share of the downsizing burden, which may start to dilute the benefits of the reorg before it has really even gotten off the ground.

At worst, failure to properly take into account and respect EU consultation obligations could derail the reorganization completely (particularly if it is time-critical) and could leave the company mired in litigation that forces it to pay damages to employees and ultimately hurts its reputation. However, the issues are not insurmountable with foresight, planning, and appropriate professional advice. The fact is that reorgs happen across the EU all the time. All it takes is a bit of planning.

Templates and Checklists for Managing Your Reorg

Timeline for your reorg

Content

Step 1: Construct the reorg's P&L

Step 2: Understand current weaknesses and strengths

Step 3: Choose from multiple options

Step 4: Get the plumbing and wiring right

Step 5: Launch, learn, and course-correct

Communications

Inform

Seek input

Engage and excite

■ Timing

Your reorg's P&L

| Step 1: Construct the reorg's P&L | Step 2: Understand current weaknesses and strengths | Step 3: Choose from multiple options | Step 4: Get the plumbing and wiring right | Step 5: Launch, learn, and course-correct |

Net benefits
($)

Net costs
($)

Time
(weeks)

Your reorg project charter

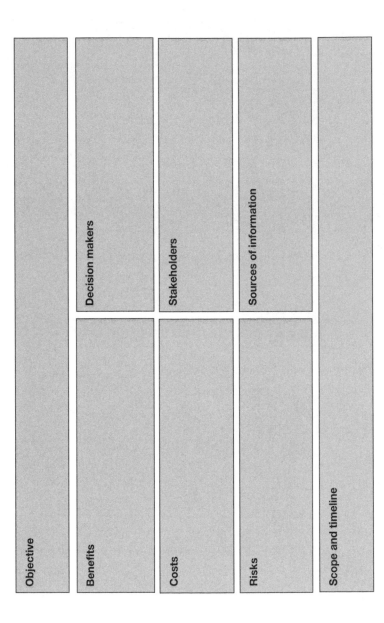

Objective

Benefits

Decision makers

Costs

Stakeholders

Risks

Sources of information

Scope and timeline

Prioritizing issues for your reorg

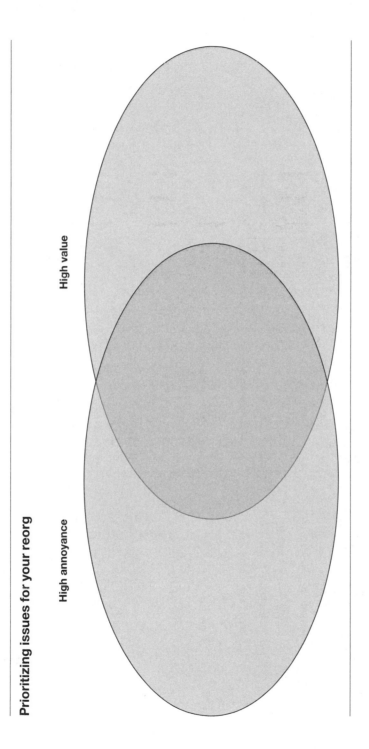

High value

High annoyance

Checklist for organization elements to cover in step 4

People

- New leaders
- Workforce numbers
- "Mass balance" per unit
- Consultation process
- Nomination process
- Recruitment
- Training

Processes

- P&L reporting
- IT system changes
  - HR
  - Finance
  - Customer/sales
  - ...
- Management processes
  - Business planning
  - Performance management
  - HR
  - ...
- Operational processes
  - Capital/R&D
  - Sales/marketing
  - Operations
  - ...

Structure

- Reporting lines
- Job titles/families
- Job grades
- Role profiles/job definitions

Work plan for step 4

People
- New leaders
- Workforce numbers
- Mass balance
- Consultation process
- Nomination process
- Recruitment
- Training

Processes
- P&L reporting
- IT systems
- Management processes
- Operational processes

Structure
- Reporting lines
- Job titles
- Job grades
- Role profiles

Time (weeks)

5,000-mile checklist for step 5

Organizational changes made

- [ ] Leaders appointed
- [ ] Staff appointed
- [ ] P&L split effectively
- [ ] Processes set up and running
- [ ] Org structures in place

Staff understand roles

Survey shows

- [ ] Staff understand objectives
- [ ] Examples that new ways of working are delivering
- [ ] Clear ideas for improvement
- [ ] Feedback on reorg

Results delivered

Outputs

- [ ] Revenues increasing
- [ ] Cost reductions tracked through to P&L

Inputs (reorg dependent)

- [ ] Sales increased
- [ ] Faster turnaround times
- [ ] New contracts in place
- [ ] Etc.

- [ ] Identify differences by geography, function, seniority

Notes

Introduction

1. Giancarlo Ghislanzoni, Stephen Heidari-Robinson, and Martin Jermiin, "Taking Organizational Design from Plan to Practice: McKinsey Global Survey Results," *McKinsey Quarterly*, 2010; Aaron De Smet and Deirdre McGinty, "The Secrets of Successful Organizational Redesigns: McKinsey Global Survey Results," *McKinsey Quarterly*, 2014.

Chapter 1

1. Giancarlo Ghislanzoni, Stephen Heidari-Robinson, and Martin Jermiin, "Taking Organizational Design from Plan to Practice: McKinsey Global Survey Results," *McKinsey Quarterly*, 2010; Aaron De Smet and Deirdre McGinty, "The Secrets of Successful Organizational Redesigns: McKinsey Global Survey Results," *McKinsey Quarterly*, 2014.

2. Other examples of reasons for reorgs are managing risk better, responding to a crisis, responding to regulatory pressure, or preparing for a divestment.

3. For further information on the challenge of managing complexity, see Julian Birkinshaw and Suzanne Heywood, "Putting Organizational Complexity in Its Place," *McKinsey Quarterly*, May 2010; Julian Birkinshaw and Suzanne Heywood, "Too Big to Manage," *Wall Street Journal*, October 26, 2009.

4. Steven Aronowitz, Aaron De Smet, and Deirdre McGinty, "Getting Organizational Redesign Right," *McKinsey Quarterly*, June 2015.

Chapter 2

1. Sarah Burgard, Lucy Kalousova, and Kristin Seefeldt, "Perceived Job Insecurity and Health: The Michigan Recession and Recovery Study," report 12-750, Population Studies Center Research Reports, University of Michigan, Ann Arbor, Michigan, January 2012. This report focuses on 519 employed workers in South Michigan during the Great Recession.

Chapter 3

1. Giancarlo Ghislanzoni, Stephen Heidari-Robinson, Suzanne Heywood, and Martin Jermiin, "How Do I Reorganize to Capture Maximum Value Quickly?" *McKinsey Insights into Organization*, 2011.

Chapter 5

1. We have a very clear view on the typical use of dotted-lines (dotted-line reporting): it generally represents a failure to define an interface properly or is the consolation prize for the loser in a contest to control staff, or is both. While multiple reporting lines are sometimes necessary, they should not be overused (as they add complexity), and when they are used, you must define both relationships. You should, for example, define everyone's roles in relation to performance management and day-to-day supervision and allocation of work. The critical thing is not just to draw a dotted line on a page and hope that people will figure out how to make it work when real-life business pressures come into play!

Chapter 6

1. Giancarlo Ghislanzoni, Stephen Heidari-Robinson, and Martin Jermiin, "Taking Organizational Design from Plan to Practice," *McKinsey Quarterly*, 2010.

2. Sarah Burgard, Jennie Brand, and James House, "Perceived Job Insecurity and Health: The Michigan Recession and Recovery Study," report 06-658, Population Studies Center Research Reports, University of Michigan, Ann Arbor, Michigan, July 2008, p. 19.

3. For example, RACI—standing for Responsible, Accountable, Consulted, and Informed.

Chapter 7

1. See William Bridges and Susan Bridges, *Managing Transitions*, 3rd ed. (New York: Da Capo Press, 2009), is a very good book about communications in times of change.

Appendix A

1. See also Suzanne Heywood, Dennis Layton, and Risto Penttinen, "A Better Way to Cut Costs," *McKinsey Quarterly*, October 2009, which included the cases described in this appendix.

Appendix C

1. Despite "Brexit" (British exit from the EU), it is unlikely that the principles of British employment law will change significantly (given the importance of case law in the British system), even if some details are changed and recourse to the EU is ended.

Index

Index

Index

Index

Acknowledgments

We decided to write this book to capture what we've learned, leading more than twenty-five major reorganizations in different sectors over the last fifteen years. We hoped to create a straight-forward, easy-to-read book—the sort of book we ourselves would have appreciated when we started doing this work. Of course, once we started, we found this goal was harder than we first thought, so we need to thank a lot of people for supporting or bearing with us through the last year. In particular, we are in debt to the following people:

- The executives who were happy for us to interview them and share their advice to others facing the same challenges: Lord John Browne, Iain Conn, John Ferraro, Lawrence Gosden, Neil Hayward, Nancy McKinstry, Hannah Meadley-Roberts, Elon Musk, Rob Rosenberg, and Alastair Swift

- Markus Schweizer for his terrific cartoons

- James Green for keeping us organized throughout this process

- David Poddington for his appendix on the legal implications of reorganizing in the EU

Acknowledgments

- Melinda Merino, our editor, for guiding us through a foreign process and for suggesting the structure of the book

- Michael Rennie, the head of McKinsey's Organization Practice, for his support and guidance

- Arne Gast, Tom Weston, and Rose Beauchamp for their detailed feedback on the manuscript

- McKinsey Organization Practice leaders we have worked with and learned from over the years: Zafer Achi, Gassan Al Kibsi, Aaron De Smet, Martin Dewhurst, Dennis Layton, Mary Meaney, Risto Penttinen, Bill Schaninger, and Warren Strickland

- Friends from our McKinsey reorg teams, especially Mark Dominic, Barry Edmonstone-West, Christopher Handscombe, Gregor Jost, and Roni Katz, from whom we learned a huge amount that is captured in this book

- Our families, in particular our very supportive spouses, Neggin and Jeremy

About the Authors

Stephen Heidari-Robinson was a leader within McKinsey & Company's Organization Practice, where he focused on energy clients and the practical implementation of reorganizations across all sectors. His work at McKinsey took him to the caravansaries of Azerbaijan, the deserts of Saudi Arabia, the megacity of Mumbai, the sewage treatment works of London, and the offices in Wichita, Kansas. Stephen has also seen organizations and reorgs from the other side: as an official in the UK Ministry of Defence, as the corporate head of a charity (Asia House), as a private equity analyst, as a vice president at Schlumberger, and, most recently, as UK Prime Minister David Cameron's advisor on energy and environment. Stephen read history (with a focus on architecture and political thought) at Oxford and the University of London, and also found time to place third in England in five thousand-meter freestyle swimming. He is a fluent Farsi speaker. He is supported by his lovely wife, Neggin, who helps him make up for his lack of personal organizational skills.

Suzanne Heywood is Managing Director, Exor Group, and sits on the boards of a number of companies, including The Economist Group and CNH Industrial, and is Deputy Chair of the Royal Opera House. From age seven to seventeen, she sailed around the world on a seventy-foot schooner called *Wavewalker*, during which time she educated herself largely by correspondence. After that she negotiated her way into university and followed that with a career that began in the UK Treasury, then at McKinsey & Company, and more recently at Exor. At McKinsey she co-led, for several years, the firm's Organization Design service line globally, and personally led McKinsey's support to more than fifteen major reorganizations in companies across different sectors. Suzanne is passionate about opera, ballet, and the visual arts, perhaps having not been able to experience them as a child. As a result, she has been involved for many years in helping arts institutions in the UK be more effective, both commercially and organizationally. She is the proud mother of three wonderful children, is writing a book about her childhood on *Wavewalker*, and still loves to travel.